The
Beauty
of
Love

ALSO BY LAURA POSADA AND JORGE POSADA

———————————

Fit Home Team: The Posada Family Guide to Health, Exercise, and Nutrition the Inexpensive and Simple Way

La familia en forma: La guía de los Posada para la salud, el ejercicio y la nutrición de una forma sencilla y económica (ebook)

The Beauty of Love

A MEMOIR OF MIRACLES, HOPE, AND HEALING

Laura Posada
and Jorge Posada

with Monica Haim

ATRIA BOOKS
New York London Toronto Sydney

ATRIA BOOKS

A Division of Simon & Schuster, Inc.
1230 Avenue of the Americas
New York, NY 10020

First Atria Books hardcover edition August 2010

ATRIA BOOKS and colophon are trademarks of Simon & Schuster, Inc.

For information about special discounts for bulk purchases,
please contact Simon & Schuster Special Sales at 1-866-506-1949
or business@simonandschuster.com.

The Simon & Schuster Speakers Bureau can bring authors to your
live event. For more information or to book an event contact the
Simon & Schuster Speakers Bureau at 1-866-248-3049 or visit our
website at www.simonspeakers.com.

Designed by Joel Avirom and Jason Snyder
Photography provided by Andrew M. Christensen and Chris Fanning

Manufactured in the United States of America

10   9   8   7   6   5   4   3   2

Library of Congress Cataloging-in-Publication Data
Posada, Jorge.
  The beauty of love : a memoir of miracles, hope, and healing / by Jorge
Posada and Laura Posada.—1st Atria Books hardcover ed.
    p. cm.
  Includes bibliographical references.
  1. Posada, Jorge Luis, 1999—Health. 2. Craniosynostoses—Patients—
Biography. 3. Craniosynostoses—Surgery—Case studies. 4. Sons—United
States—Biography. 5. Posada, Jorge—Family. 6. Posada, Laura—Family.
7. Love. I. Posada, Laura. II. Title.
  RJ482.C73P66 2010
  618.92'00430922—dc22
                                                                    2010018962

ISBN 978-1-4391-0308-1
ISBN 978-1-4391-4967-6 (ebook)

For Jorge, our son, who taught us how to love; for every family in the world forced to endure a crisis through illness; for every child that we have had the honor to meet and help through the Foundation; and for those whom we hope to help in the future

———————————————

Contents

Foreword

BY JOE TORRE

S witch-hitting, the ability to swing from both sides of the plate, is impressive and rare in baseball, but also metaphorically, in real life; so it is as refreshing as it is inspiring when you know a man who can do them both. After all, switch-hitting essentially reflects the art of adaptation and the mystery of flexibility, attributes that undoubtedly make for a healthy ball game *and* a balanced state of being. I remember the morning Jorge Posada asked me for the day off, for what would be the first of eight major surgeries that his infant son would have to undergo to treat a life-threatening illness that doctors diagnosed when the baby was just ten days old. Here was a man in the prime of his career, a rising star, who over time would become one of the most popular catchers in Yankee history, with more runs batted in since 2000 (the year of his son's first surgery!) than any other catcher in baseball.

In one hand he held the fate of his escalating success; in the other, the emphatic belief and unshakable faith that his son would somehow, despite the severity of the disease, be okay. Where did he get the emotional wherewithal and stamina to juggle such extremes, and how did he have the strength to be not only the player *we* needed him to be, but the husband and father that his family needed even more at home?

Well, it's really no mystery, because you see, this is what Jorge Posada is all about—switch-hitting his way through life's ups and downs with grace, confidence, and the kind of nobility that turns an ordinary man into a role model. During what were probably the most emotionally challenging years of his life, as his firstborn son was in and out of the hospital, with one elaborate surgery after another, Jorge managed to: become the only major-league catcher to ever hit .330 or better, with 40 doubles, 20 home runs, and 85 RBIs in a season; play in six All-Star Games; and along with Yogi Berra become the only other Yankee catcher to hit 30 home runs in a season. These stats are impressive as it is—now imagine achieving them all in the face of serious family turmoil, uncertain futures, life, and death.

And as we know, behind every great man there is often a great woman, so it's no surprise that between Jorge and his lovely wife, Laura, the Posada family has emerged as a beacon of strength, integrity, philanthropy, and love—a model for families everywhere who might be battling with illness and pain and a human testament to the power of patience and perseverance.

It has been a pleasure and privilege to know and work with Jorge; and though I've been the one managing him all these years, he has been one of the men responsible for our Yankee championships. Jorge Posada truly exemplifies what it takes to be a role model, whether playing the game of baseball or the game of life.

Introduction

I know I will survive, I'm a fighter.
—SHIRLEY CHISHOLM

Laura Posada:

The night before our son Jorge Luis's first surgery, while everyone was asleep, I locked myself in the bathroom and took a long, hot shower. There, in the heavy steam, my tired mind and body, unable to pretend any longer, finally gave in. I fell down on my knees and collapsed there to cry. I cried so much, my tears and the water pouring down on me, as I prayed for my son not to die. All I could do was replay the horrible string of words the doctors all used when talking about the surgery: *fronto-orbital advancement . . . cranial vault remodeling . . . three blood transfusions . . . must be type O negative . . . a complicated surgery that could last up to eleven hours . . . delicate . . . the skull needs to be opened from ear to ear . . . there is the risk of brain damage . . . they have to reshape the bones, reinstall them, and then sew him back up.* All of this to my nine-month-old. How could I not imagine that he was going to die? It crossed my mind that this might be the last time I would ever get to put my son to sleep, and the thought of losing him became tangible, stinging me deeply in the center of my soul.

When we awoke the next day, it was scorching outside, the heat and steam relentlessly pressing down on New York the way they know how to in early August. It was only 6 A.M., and you could already feel how hot the day was going to be. The operation had been scheduled early in the morning, purposely to avoid Jorge having to sign autographs in the hospital or deal with any paparazzi, since he was so well known and recognized in New York.

When we arrived at the hospital, we sat in a little waiting room before they called us in, huddled all together but no one really saying anything, the weight of the future pushing us down into the earth. Jorge and I looked at each other and said no words—but in that silence communicated to each other that we had to do what we had to do.

We were told that one parent was allowed to accompany the baby into the operating room where they would prepare him, and Jorge and I had decided that I should be the one to do it. No task has ever daunted me more, but I agreed and watched my family (Jorge, his father, and my parents) shrink smaller and smaller as my baby and I were escorted down an ugly, white-gray hospital corridor toward the OR. I was now alone in the world, alone with my son, who could not possibly understand any of it and who would likely one day turn to me for an explanation.

The operating room was set up for the surgery, and I was instructed to put on a full bunny suit with my head and feet fully covered to maintain sterility. There were photographs and X-rays around the room. A tray lined with a light blue paper cloth was equipped with all varieties of meticulously placed surgical tools, all of them looking to me like torture devices, gleaming ominously under the hot surgical lights. Surgeons and nurses shuffled about, whispering in unintelligible codes, their intent eyes looking serious through the tiny spaces in their masks. They put Jorge Luis on the operating table, but he wouldn't stop crying. I was actually the one who put him down on the table, and honestly I don't know how I was able to let go. A nurse gently placed a mask on his face until he slowly fell silent and then just lay there totally still. They escorted me out of the room, explaining that it would be at least twelve to thirteen hours before I would see him again. It would be the longest amount of time that I'd ever been separated from him since the moment of his birth, not to mention *where* I was leaving him, and under what circumstances. For the first time I would not be the one to address his needs and make him feel better. Against everything that felt normal and right to me, I was forced to relinquish my responsibility for my son to a team of doctors, forcing myself to believe that their expertise would eclipse the feelings of doubt that would bubble up for every single moment of those thirteen hours. Never mind the obvious trauma of having to see my firstborn son sedated on that cold steel operating table—but the thought of this moment being one of his first experiences in the world totally and utterly crushed me.

And so began my first real encounter with motherhood.

For a new parent, one of the most glorious things in existence is the tiny spectacle of a beautiful newborn child looking up at you, his perfect little features fresh and soft, his infectious smile representing for you a brand new world of hope and possibilities. In that momentary flash, we come to understand the power of creation, our roles within it, and the divine magic built into the experience of such profound kinship. We inhale the sweet aromas of newness and innocence, realizing with each breath that moves into our center that our lives indeed have new meaning. Many would say that this moment is the quintessential peak of life, the first magical encounter with your very own blood, a unique and primal meeting that has the power to awaken your sense of purpose and fuel your ability to love.

But what would happen if the beautiful face was not perfect? What would happen if those early days that you had envisioned would radiate with the happy glow of sweet pastel pinks and baby blues became instead cast with a dismal and mysterious gray that only seemed to darken with each day that passed? What would happen if you were to look down at your newborn and, rather than experience the long-awaited surge of bliss you'd always imagined, you instead encountered your own sense of dread bubbling up from within? *What happens when the illusion of perfection is shattered right from the start?*

These were some of the painful questions that haunted our world when our son, Jorge Luis, was diagnosed with a skull deformation at just ten days old, a shocking revelation that would radically alter the course of our lives. From one day to the next we abruptly went from being the joyful young couple, strong and successful, smiling proudly to throngs of adoring fans and waiting in bliss for the arrival of our firstborn son, to a couple of terrified, helpless parents with no concrete answers and only the looming prospect of a very sick baby to contend with. Talk about curveballs.

With the birth of our son came a dark and looming silence, a fear of the unknown, and what felt like a knife stab to the heart. Words like "craniotomy," "facial deformities," and "neurological problems" were thrown at us, and every moment became an exercise in emotional survival. Each year brought a new surgery and each surgery a new aftermath, laden with complications and even more questions. Our lives became defined by the grim new reality and subsequent progress of our precious son's health, and our collective mission became to understand and conquer his disease.

But because this took place almost a decade ago, way before the word "Google" was considered a verb, information was scarce and there was little we could do to learn much about this understudied illness. We felt alone in our suffering and terrified by our helplessness. So many aspects of our son's condition seemed impossible to digest, starting with the multiple surgeries that would be involved in treating it. Our doctors and surgeons became saviors, entrusted with the deepest, most vulnerable parts of us every single time we let our child go under the knife.

We quickly had to come to terms with the fact that the mysterious illness would be an ever-shifting phenomenon, one that would elicit much anguish and little relief. On the one hand, we would never quite know how things were going to develop, but on the other hand, we had to be ready to respond, with courage, to pretty much anything that arose; and being that this very nebulous "anything" was occurring to an adorable, helpless infant—our first baby—the whole thing seemed both incredibly scary and ridiculously unfair.

We would lie awake at night trying to grasp how this could be happening to a creature so small; wondering what we had done wrong, what we could have possibly done to cause this, and worried ourselves crazy about how it was all going to work out. For years, we woke up to countless mornings of not knowing what the day ahead would hold. We felt the massive and intimidating doors of so many operating rooms swing open and closed behind us, with our tiny little man on the other side.

We shuffled along so many icy hospital corridors in agony and anticipation, praying for miracle after miracle, as our friends and families watched, praying with us.

Our son's well-being became our unspoken mission, fueled by what became our unshakable determination to stay positive. We decided to face the condition head-on, determined to go through each step of the process with grace and fortitude, and were at last able to find that strength deep in the sweet brown eyes of Jorge Luis, who would look up at us after every surgery, reminding us silently to show our resilience. Given the fact that he was just a baby, his health problem was not exactly something he could understand rationally; nonetheless, he would seem to boldly look the world dead in the eye, accept his circumstances and reality, always poised like a little adult—and after eight surgeries and countless doctor visits, exams, checkups, and tests, he *never once complained.* His innocent little smile became the symbol of our hope, and each day in his company would bring us a new and invaluable lesson in endurance, patience, perseverance, and countless other virtues that we would have to call upon and hold close. We realized that despite the challenges of such a disease, it would always be our duty to give our son the best life that we could— and we dedicated ourselves to the pursuit of his happiness. In this journey, we discovered a love so pure and real, a love that had nothing to do with our egos and everything to do with our family.

Just like that, our sense of "what matters" was turned on its head, an unexpected paradigm shift that ultimately brought us endless transformation. After what seemed like an eternity spent in total despair, something finally clicked, and we realized that our burden could also be a blessing and that our experience could actually matter in the bigger picture of this disease. We looked far past the horizon of our own reality and found a way to change our suffering into initiative. Our role as awareness builders for this illness gave new meaning to our lives, and we began to see our own experience of sorrow as a tremendous opportunity—a chance not only to educate the medical community about this disease but also to help those afflicted with the condition in every possible way we could. And with that realization, our lives would change forever.

This book is a testament of love, our personal account of the power of family unity when faced with uncertainty and pain. It is meant to inspire families dealing with any type of illness, reminding them that hope dies last and that the possibility of solutions and support will always exist.

Through our own narrative, along with the various insights, ideas, and comments of many of the close friends, doctors, and family members who were very much part of the experience, we have compiled our story, a story of hope, faith, and fierce positivity—one that we sincerely believe expresses the beauty in love. Because as we understand it now, true beauty lives deep in the soul and can be properly appreciated only when you begin to truly love.

There is not a day that goes by that we do not thank the universe for the blessing of our son. He, along with our little daughter, is the absolute love and light of our lives—but he also represents the true meaning of valor, strength, and the power of family when the chips are down. In this way, Jorge Luis is more than just our son—he is also our total inspiration and a delicious little miracle. *The Beauty of Love* is the story of our family's greatest victory, and how, through much perseverance, we won it with our hearts.

PART I

Lessons in Luck

Other things may change us,
but we start and end with the family.
—ANTHONY BRANDT

CHAPTER I

Raised on Roots

Jorge Posada:

My wife, Laura, and I have always been your classic glass–half-full, happy-face-on, hopes-up sort of people. We were always grateful for our bountiful lives, which consistently felt complete with the blessings of family love and wonderful closeness, the kind of built-in, homegrown kinship that made for good times and effortless bliss. Our dinner tables were always heaping with warm tropical food and even warmer company, a conscious sense of togetherness that fed us both with security, confidence, tradition, and, of course, love. We were raised to be strong, healthy kids in strong, healthy families with solid genes, built to work, play, perform, and consistently win. That's the stuff we were made of.

Our families, like many Latino families, were *always there.* Without fail they would sit smiling proudly in the bleachers at all of our sporting events, at all the holiday events, backstage at our talent shows, and at every little thing in between. They were our people, and we were their loves. They were our role models, and we were their dreams. They taught us the importance of creating goals and the significance of fighting for them with all of our hearts. They gave every ounce of themselves to us, to our well-being, and we learned everything we know directly from them.

Reflecting today on the story of our lives, it's hard not to think back on how it all used to be when we were just starting to make sense of the world ourselves. As for myself, I was born in 1971, on the seventeenth day of August, which, as I understand, is in the astrological sign of the lion. I was fortunate enough to come into this world in the beautiful barrio of Santurce, on the northeast coast of the island of Puerto Rico, where we had five kilometers of white sand beaches and warm and magical aquamarine waters delivered directly from the Atlantic Ocean. Where I came from, the sun was always shining bright, the markets were always hot and bustling with the smells of fresh herbs and plentiful produce, and the people—coastal to the core—were all smiles all the time. Everyone was accustomed to the familiar, intimate warmth of family, laughter, and the quintessential ideals of pure island living. It was the kind of place with many blessings and few concerns, one that gave liberty to my Cuban father along with hope for a bright future for the entire family. It was also the place that gave us one of the first teams for Puerto Rico's professional baseball leagues—and, for as long as I can remember, the sport ran through my veins along with my blood.

My mother, Tamara, was born in Santo Domingo in the Dominican Republic and moved to Puerto Rico in 1961 at the age of eighteen. Three years later she met my father, Jorge, Sr., a total Habanero from Cuba who left the island in 1968 after eight years under the rule of Fidel Castro. He had escaped in a tobacco container ship that took him to Greece, New York, and later Spain, where he would play baseball for six months as he waited for his papers to clear so that he could travel to Puerto Rico. When he finally did arrive, he organized the "League of Novatos" and gradually became a trusted authority on baseball on the island, which he is to this day.

As I understand it, when my parents first met, my mother was working at an apothecary shop my father used to visit as a pharmaceutical vendor. As the story goes, one day he arrived at the store and my mother noticed him while he was telling someone a story of recently having been robbed. For some reason she thought it would be hilarious to hide his briefcase, which she proceeded to do without pause for concern, and my father, of course, went out of his mind searching for his case, unable to believe the horrendous state of his luck, perhaps thinking that he had fallen victim to a curse of bad fortune. My mother finally showed mercy, coyly confessed the prank, and returned his briefcase—which is how their romance began. They have since been married for thirty-nine years and to this day live in the house where my younger sister, Michelle, and I were raised by their hands.

I remember always being a bit protective of my sister. I recall her first day of school and the pride I felt as her older brother, knowing innately that it was my duty to ensure her safety and contentment as much as I could. I would keep a close watch on her, and in turn she was always one of my most zealous fans out there on the ballpark bleachers. No matter what, I knew that my sweet sister's smiling face in the crowd was something I would consistently see in my peripheral view on almost every field I ever played on. Despite the fact that she was somewhat timid and had a particular earnestness about her, I could always pick up on her genuine enthusiasm for my progress as an athlete, and I carried that feeling of family support with me to all of my games.

Michelle Posada (Jorge's sister):

Jorge and I were never the kind of siblings who argued or fought; we were always affectionate with each other, and he was endlessly protective of me. One time in the fourth grade I remember that someone stole the last stamp from my favorite series in a collection, and Jorge made it his personal mission to go retrieve that precious stamp for me, by any means necessary, putting himself on the line for me without thinking twice. He always watched over me, and I always felt safe and unconditionally loved in his care.

My parents were from the old school, relentlessly Latino and ever strict about their rules. My dad was your classic textbook workaholic, juggling three jobs but always carrying a serious work ethic from one to the next. He was a worker in the truest sense of the word, a believer in the notion of accountability and the power of discipline. There was always a little bit of tension in the house but always just as much love and encouragement—a healthy balance of rules and closeness that kept everyone both happy and on their toes. The family bond we shared was a given and not something necessarily expressed in hugs and kisses, but nonetheless solid as a rock.

As early as I can remember, my whole family showed a profound commitment to my development as a baseball player, always displaying a show of support that would follow me from ballpark to ballpark, fueling my game with positive energy time and again. It was almost as if each one had a role to play at every game: my father as the rigorous coach, my mother as the provider of treats and encouragement, and my sister as my all-around confidante whom I loved to have around. Our family life in many ways revolved around baseball and all of the rigors that come with it, and today I can sincerely appreciate how much this close-knit entourage of kin became my foundation, giving so much of themselves to my cause as an athlete.

Over the years, my father, as well as my uncle Leo, became known as among the finest Cuban baseball players in their day; my dad played in the minor leagues, and Leo became the

Tamara Posada (Jorge's mother):

Jorge was quietly restless, always respectful, and incredibly warm. He was a timid child, and the only thing he *did* talk or seemingly think about was baseball. It was as if he had a baseball bat and a glove etched on his forehead from birth. He didn't like to wake up for school during the week, but on Saturdays he would wake up with the roosters, because he knew it was his day to practice playing baseball. In third grade he told his teacher that he didn't need to learn English, because when he grew up he was going to be a professional baseball player, and he would be able to learn English then. Jorge studied in a military academy from the time he was a little boy, which, of course, gave him a lot of discipline. My husband was also quite strict. The kids were not allowed to loiter in the streets; they were expected to behave with integrity at all times.

everyday right fielder for the Kansas City A's in the early sixties. As for myself, given my father's fervor for the game, the baseball bat and glove were essentially introduced to me right along with my milk bottle, making the game not only my passion but also very much my priority.

Growing up, I was always a little kid, on the short and skinny side, and my poor mother suffered interminably because I really didn't like to eat. The doctor said I was anemic, and everyone seemed to keep a close eye on my growth and physical development. I was always the smallest in the class, so sports (even baseball) were always a bit harder for me, and there were always a lot of people around me who definitely showed more talent. But I loved the game so much and I wanted it so much that I just kept working and pushing forward.

Michelle Posada (Jorge's sister):

Since he was a kid, we all knew deep down that Jorge would turn out to be a baseball player, or *pelotero*, as we say in Puerto Rico. He also always knew it, and would say it to everyone proudly and surely. Baseball was his entire life. I have distinct memories of seeing him in his room wearing a glove, bouncing a baseball against the wall and catching it, in some kind of baseball trance, perhaps daydreaming of the glorious days that would come. He would stay in that rhythm for hours. As his little sister, I grew up moving from baseball field to baseball field, because every time Jorge had a game, which seemed like every other week, we would all attend as a matter of course. It was clear that my father had a plan for Jorge's athletic career, and it was also evident that our support was a necessary element to ensure that my brother would always feel our love and encouragement and therefore perform at his best. We were always his team, and he was always our star.

When I was twelve, my father was slated to play a softball game in New Jersey and we got to visit Yankee Stadium, where, for the first time, I saw Don Mattingly and Dave Winfield playing live, in the flesh, right there before me. I know something hit me that day in that magnificent park, a magical place so full of talent, hard work, and lore, and I distinctly remember turning to my mother and sister and saying with the assuredness of a full-grown adult, "I'm gonna play baseball here someday." It was one of those defining moments in my life when I learned something profound about myself that I would carry around forever, and from that moment on, my goal and desire to become a professional baseball player would essentially drive my sense of purpose.

CHAPTER 2

Family Matters

A son is a son till he takes a wife,
a daughter is a daughter all of her life.
—IRISH PROVERB

Laura Posada (Jorge's wife):

I n Hato Rey, the more commercial district of Puerto Rico where I grew up, our family enjoyed a privileged life in the area famous for a stretch of banks and skyscrapers known as the Golden Mile. Life indeed seemed cast in a golden aura of closeness and love, and I know I can speak for my siblings when I say that we had it all: giving parents, a lovely home, recreation of all varieties, and the kind of positive disposition that makes a kid believe she is capable of pretty much anything.

My mother's father passed away when she was just three years old, and her mother (my grandmother) married a second time. The youngest of seven siblings, my mother went to college in Scranton, Pennsylvania, an unusual destination for a Latina and even more so in that era. She finished school and returned to Puerto Rico to work for a dairy products company. She met my father, who used to frequent the same lunchtime restaurant, as he worked as a hospital administrator nearby. They recognized each other from their teen years in Hato Rey, and so began a regular lunch routine that would eventually lead to their marriage. Because her father had passed away when she was so young, my father essentially stepped in as the dominant male figure in her life.

Our father, ever the family man, was raised among seven brothers and sisters, and as for our grandfather, he was actually the mayor of the town. My siblings and I grew up with twenty-one first cousins from one side and another twenty-something on the other, so our family gave new meaning to the word "get-together." A small family gathering meant at least fifty people, piles of robust Latin provisions, saucy music, and endless supplies of hugs and laughter to go around. There was never a sense of dullness or quiet; our family time was laced with a celebratory sense of unity and jubilation at every opportunity. Everywhere I went in Puerto Rico, I was sure to run into at least two cousins. I honestly believe that this understanding of family, and knowing that we were never really alone, created and shaped our strong personalities. It gave us all a sense of belonging, confidence, and values. Our parents raised us to stare at our goals with the eyes of the tiger, a can-do sense of motivation and drive that fueled everything we attempted to do.

Our father was a driven, business-minded guy; and our mother was what they call, in Spanish, *pan de Dios,* an expression that describes a sweet, gentle soul and literally means "bread of God." She was the kind of woman whose most ominous threat was "Wait until your father gets home." And she was right to warn us, as my father was from the old guard of Latin machismo, where raising the voice was par for the course at home and the men reigned supreme as the kings of their castles. Everything was in their domain and purview, a steady undercurrent of built-in respect, a cultural common denominator of the Latin world.

My father reigned over our household with endless amounts of love but with a steady arsenal of rules that shaped and defined the stern atmosphere in our home. Our friends, for example, knew not to call our house past nine at night, and if by chance they happened to call at 9:01 P.M., they would be politely told to call back the next day at a more reasonable hour. And even when they called within the permissible hours, my father would go as far as to correct their grammar, demanding that they speak properly and greet him with respect. By the time I was old enough to go out—*if* my father approved of the person I was to go out with—my suitor in question would have to park in our driveway, get out of the car, ring the doorbell, come into our house, greet my entire family, and undergo a full cross-examination by my father, who would, of course, remind the gentleman caller of my impending curfew. When we would complain to our mother of our father's tyranny, she would remind us that we should be grateful that we had a father at all.

We also had a Cuban nanny who had had five miscarriages and never had children of her own, so she and I bonded intensely. I loved her like a mother. She was the one who taught me how to pray and about etiquette when dealing with boys, and she was one of the people in my life who always inspired me with a sense of tenderness.

Despite being a female, I always basked in what I considered to be prime status as the baby of my house, five years my sister's junior and four years younger than my brother. As a family, we would always play board games and cards, and, as in everything else we ventured to do, excelling even at these seemingly meaningless diversions was considered a high priority. At home, losing equaled failure, so (not unlike Jorge) I always had to work a bit harder as the little one, relying perhaps on some extra sense of drive to be the best and do everything with perfection. Extracurricular activities were permissible only if my grades were good, and my parents were steadfast in their belief that education was fundamental above all else. Our collective sense of healthy competitiveness underscored everything that we did at home, which I believe propelled us all to crave success down the line.

I too was ever the ambitious athlete, competing in everything from volleyball and basketball to softball and even track—and in high school I was the "female athlete of the year" for several years consecutively. I considered myself a fierce competitor; I was determined not only to perform at my maximum but also to always win. Not winning was never an option, and I carried this ferocious zeal to every game that I played. When I was around eleven years old, I wanted to play volleyball with the older girls and decided to show up to their practice. I was the smallest and youngest, and when I tried to play everyone laughed at me. Shot down, totally rejected, and feeling that I had failed for the first time, I went home boiling with shame and instantly said to my brother, "You better teach me how to play volleyball." For the remainder of that year he and I practiced together every single day, and after much persistence, in high school I was ultimately nominated "Miss Volleyball," captain of the volleyball team, and MVP almost every year. We considered this triumph as a collective family mission, my brother and I, which is exactly what our family was all about.

And my aspirations did not stop at sports: from the age of fourteen, I also modeled, tap-danced, and performed in television commercials, fancying myself the kind of person who could do it all, a Renaissance kid of the truest kind. I was named "most likely to be famous" in our high school yearbook and was elected as Miss Junior and Miss Senior in sports for two years back-to-back. I was pretty, popular, and personable, all of the makings of what I then considered to be a winner. A guardian angel was smiling upon me, I would always think to myself, gratefully armed with a sense of confidence that seemed to effortlessly guide my way.

Manuel Mendez (Laura's father):

*I*t was always important to me that my children have a sense of ritual, and sitting together at dinner was at the top of that list. The family dinner was sacred, not to be interfered with, a time without television, diversions, or any other such nonsense that would deter from this special family moment. The only thing that mattered at the dinner table was the steaming plate of homemade arroz con habichuelas under your nose and the endearing stories of relatives shared over the delicious home-cooked food.

I was a demanding father, but I also knew how to reward my kids. They were allowed and encouraged to play all varieties of board games and participate in whatever activity their hearts might desire—but they were expected to retire early in the evening, wake up at the next dawn, and excel in school. I never tolerated cursing or slang, and I always pushed for things like punctuality and respect for the family. At night, I would sing to them:

> *Vamos a la cama* [let's go to bed]
> *Tenemos que descansar* [we have to rest]
> *Para que mañana* [so that tomorrow]
> *Podamos madrugar* [we can get up early]

> **Good grades were paid with cash money. If they got As they would earn a certain amount; Bs, of course, got them a lesser amount. Cs and Ds were simply not worth anything—and an F was just not fathomable. Call it what you want, but it worked. My kids were always driven, competitive, and sharp, and they would all carry their sense of accomplishment and desire for success throughout their lives.**

Safe to say, my parents' efforts paid off. My sister took her pristine 98 average straight to Harvard and became a world-renowned doctor in the field of breast surgery—not an easy task for a Latina in the early 1990s. My brother, a can-do guy in his own right, earned a degree in biomedical engineering from Boston University, and followed that up with an MBA at Northwestern, at its Kellogg School of Business. As for myself, I graduated from high school in 1989 and went off to Loyola University in New Orleans, where I enrolled for a BA in communications and then attended law school. I would later return to Puerto Rico to take the state and federal bar, to accomplish my goal of one day being among Puerto Rico's fiercest and feistiest female attorneys.

CHAPTER 3

Game On

Discipline is remembering what you want.
—DAVID CAMPBELL

Jorge:

When I look back, I realize that my dad, ever the zealous coach, made a minicareer out of molding my game. Given his own experience in and passion for the sport, he somehow channeled all of his own personal fervor into the advancement of my skills on the field. Perhaps seeing some talent in me, or maybe just wanting to live vicariously through the opportunity of my youth, he became intent on furthering my game. It was less like a father-son exchange and more like a coach-protégé scenario, where each day would bring another chance to add more refinements to my technique. It started with him pushing me to lose my aluminum bat for a wooden one when I was only eight years old and making me play that way for the entire next decade. Not only that, but up until I was five, I was a natural right-handed hitter, until one day my father suggested that I start swinging with my left arm. I then batted exclusively from the left side until my thirteenth birthday. Then one day, with a left-handed pitcher on the hill, my father told me to take my swings right-handed. I did as he instructed, and, just as he had hoped, I began stinging the ball. These early attempts to evolve me into a switch-hitter would steadily improve my game. In high school I tried to participate in many different sports, including volleyball, track, and basketball, but my dad would literally pull me off the basketball court and encourage me to focus solely on baseball. He was on a mission, and I knew better than to argue with or question him. It was clear that he had a plan, and though sometimes he was hard on me, instinctively I knew to trust him. After all, the man did have years of experience and an uncanny sense of knowing what would work well on the field. It worked out in my favor, because in high school I was named All-Star player as shortstop in the 1988–1989 season. Truth be told, my father single-handedly helped to shape me into the player I ultimately became, and in many ways, I was his personal little project.

I'll never forget the time he handed me a gallon of paint with a deadpan look on his face and told me to go outside and paint a wall. He did not give an explanation as to why I had to do this, nor did he ask me if I even wanted to. It was a one-way instruction, the kind that doesn't leave any room for objection or refutation. I was expected to comply, and of course I did. Needless to say, painting a wall was the last thing I wanted to do that afternoon because back then I could hardly appreciate the lesson he wanted to impart: the power of the work ethic and the importance of always being up for a physical challenge. In the end, it became clear that the paint job had nothing to do with home refurbishment and everything to do with making me stronger.

I remember another time when he arranged for a truck to dump a pile of dirt outside our house in Santurce. Despite the fact that I was only twelve years old and skinny as a rail, my ever-stringent father demanded that I move the entire load of soil, using a wheelbarrow, to the backyard, to level the earth below

Tamara (Jorge's mother):

I pushed him too. On Saturdays, near the park where Jorge practiced, there was a cafeteria, where it was my duty to purchase sweets for our son, for the sole purpose of rewarding him when he played well and to keep him batting strong. We would spend the whole nine innings like that, swapping hard hits for sweet treats. Call it what you will, but I always wanted my son to be the best, because I knew that he could be. He always showed incredible discipline and steady focus, and it was a joy to watch him display these virtues while he played.

the house. I was mercilessly forced to work on the project every day for several hours, which I did, despite not fully understanding why this horrendous chore was being asked of twelve-year-old me. Though I'm sure I resented being assigned to the task back then, only now can I truly appreciate why my father made me do it: to help strengthen my grip, shoulders, and legs—all of which would, in turn, strengthen my game. We were gradually becoming like the Puerto Rican equivalent of Mr. Miyagi in the movie *The Karate Kid* and his karate-learning protégé, "Daniel son"—a symbiotic relationship built on the virtues of discipline, respect, trust, and progress. My father's steady training and support would shadow every move I made as an athlete, and as I grew older I'd begin to understand his seemingly random demands as all being part of his effort to help me succeed.

But my parents were not the only ones encouraging and inspiring me out there on the field, as I had many baseball heroes, not the least of whom were Thurman Munson, the All-Star catcher for the New York Yankees, and Roberto Clemente. Ironically, both of those men were killed in plane crashes, but their legacies would leave an incredible impact on me as I continued down my path as an aspiring player. I had many other role models: George Brett, Don Mattingly, Barry Larkin, Andy Van Slyke, and Tony Fernandez were all standout athletes whom I would try to emulate as I continued to develop my own style.

Toward the end of high school, as my father's tireless training really began to take hold, I managed to pique the interest of Fred

Frickie, an American baseball coach who had somehow heard that I was a talented shortstop. With his referral, I wound up attending Calhoun Community College in Decatur, Alabama, after signing a letter of intent and being offered a scholarship to play for the school's team. Though it was no walk in the park to be one of the few Latinos in what seemed like the whitest, most rural place I had ever encountered, I was there to play ball and in fact played well enough to get the attention of Leon Wurth, a scout for the New York Yankees, who in 1990 saw me play against a junior college from Tennessee and convinced the New York Yankees to recruit me. Maybe it was because I still considered myself a rookie, or maybe because my English did not feel polished enough—but for whatever reason, I decided to hold out on joining the Yankees then and instead played with a summer-league team in Alabama, with Mr. Wurth watching closely. Back then I could not possibly understand the prospect of the momentous journey that could unfold for me as a member of this legendary team. Still, I somehow knew that I was on the right track and felt honored to have even been considered.

With every day that passed, I became more and more enamored with the game; however, it was not entirely clear to my mentors, or to me, which position I would be best suited for. Leon Wurth one day suggested I try catching, and though at first it felt unfamiliar and even challenging, I also knew that I was starting to zero in on my true potency and strongest talent. After my final year at Calhoun, on the recommendation of Mr. Wurth, I reopened my discussions with the New York Yankees and officially signed with them in the twenty-fourth round of the 1990 amateur spring draft. I knew that I was on the brink of a life-changing step, though at the time I could not possibly understand the magnitude of playing among such a solid and inspiring group of players.

During my first year with the Yankees, I was placed mostly infield, but after the first season I began playing solely as a catcher in the Fall Instructional League, where I was able to steadily improve and work my way upward. As my base hits and runs went up, so too did the Yankees' faith and trust in me, and by 1994 I was beyond thrilled to be heading toward the major leagues. I was doing really well with the team, the kind of progress that ultimately earned me a promotion to the Triple-A Columbus Clippers of the International League, where, for the first time, I got to play alongside the likes of Derek Jeter and Andy Pettitte, making my major-league debut in 1995. Some of my most valuable friendships were made during these years, the kinds of bonds that I will likely keep alive for the rest of my life. As a kid in Puerto Rico, I would never have imagined the potential scope of what began as a childhood hobby. I always knew I wanted to be a professional baseball player, but it did not necessarily occur to me that it would happen this fast or at this level. Those were some of the most exciting moments of my life, the kinds of memories that for me as a young boy could only seem like far-reaching fantasies. It all felt incredibly surreal, yet there I was making it all happen— and there it was all happening to me.

CHAPTER 4

Youthful Illusions

Laura:

Loyola was a major party school in a major party city. From the moment my parents left me there at the ripe young age of seventeen, for the first time, I was able to taste the sweetness of pure liberation, of course loving and savoring every last little bit of it. After years of so many restrictions at home, I could not believe that my mother and father were actually going to let me live on my own, far away from them, away from their strict code of conduct and their endless expectations. I suppose that meant that they trusted me, which also allowed me to go into this new chapter with confidence. I wanted to make them proud as much as I wanted to excel personally, but there was still no denying that I felt like a bird just freed from its cage. I somehow knew right away that I was about to embark on what I imagined would be the most glorious of my glory years. My mother and father, who would continue to surprise me, were endlessly forthcoming with their generosity, leaving me the option never to have to work while I was in school. They also left me provided to the brim with every possible necessity I might require, from credit cards and petty cash to a car and enough furniture to fill my new dorm room. They went as far as stocking my brand-new refrigerator with fresh food and cold beverages, leaving no detail unaccounted for, ensuring that their baby girl would be okay. As far as I was concerned, I was living the perfect life.

At Loyola, I remained focused on my schoolwork but spent plenty of time socializing and milking the vibrant New Orleans experience. Every moment felt like a new little blessing. The city always felt alive with music and jubilation, and just having the opportunity to live in such a culturally juicy environment was thrilling—especially for a girl from Hato Rey, Puerto Rico, whose father ruled the household with old-school austerity. New Orleans was the kind of city where you could always hear music or drums in the distance, where the smell of fritters and seafood lingered in the air, and where people's eyes told their entire stories. It was a city laced with lore and myths, a place where you'd imagine there were secrets laden in every crevice and where the local women "knew things." Cultural diversity gave color and dimension to the city, with elements of France, jazz culture, and Creole all mingling to form a distinct New Orleans vibe. It was not a "regular" city by any means and instead radiated the kind of magic that you read about in some of the best novels. It was like a movie set, except that it was real, and for the next few years I would have total freedom to explore it.

My college years, for this reason, also served as a major decompression from the rigorous demands of my adolescence. During that time I answered to no one's rules but my own. Never before had I been left to my own devices, to roam wildly, to experiment with abandon. I was totally free, without a care in the world. I was hoping to start paving the way for an amazing career ahead of me and many years in which to milk my new-found independence.

College was a perfect place for me to test the sense of balance I had always envisioned for myself. Having had experience as an actress and model, I cared about staying in shape and looking my personal best, but I was equally concerned with making excellent grades, attending inspiring classes, and getting as thorough an education as possible. I did not want to be known for being pretty—I wanted to be known for being *complete*. I was there to give my all from every perspective, to be social and smart, and to tap into my inner superstar for what I thought of as the greatest years of my life.

There were lots of Puerto Ricans around, so I felt right at home at Loyola. But I was also far away enough from home to carve out my own individual space, without having to look over my shoulder for my parents' approval. Like college kids in every generation, I felt that this new independence would allow me to further shape my identity as a young woman, by letting me exist in my own terms, with only my goals directing me. I wanted to stay active all the time, engaged with every aspect of my new world, from my school curriculum to the steady flow of boys I dated to partying like a true professional. At one point, I began hosting Latin-night parties on Saturday nights at a local dance club and earning all of the cash from the door. It was my way of bringing a little slice of Puerto Rico to New Orleans, which ended up being a total sensation for the local Hispanics who craved the sassy sound of salsa and wanted to reconnect. Lines of party people would form at the door, everyone happy and sweaty and just wanting to get down—and I could not get over the fact that I was the one who had ignited it all. I was so proud of myself for having the initiative and drive to create something like this and was delighted to see how quickly a good idea can really come into fruition.

I fancied myself a total maverick and had the hearty social life and perfect grades to prove it. I was determined to work hard and play even harder, using all of the practiced motivation from my youth to excel. Somehow or another I managed to party like a rock star *and* keep my grades up, further proving to myself that I really was capable of anything. My university years continued to shape my core desire to become a total superwoman.

Perhaps I was a bit on the selfish side—albeit in the way that I believed all modern women ought to be—but when I gave thought to the future, the picture that emerged in my mind featured predominantly *me.* When people asked me what I was going to do with my life, I would proudly claim that I would become a sports agent and/or an entertainment lawyer. I envisioned myself as some kind of successful, powerful, unstoppable femme fatale—an intellectual seductress with equal parts wiles and brain. I saw myself as independent, sexy, and totally capable. I did not want to have to depend on anyone; and all I *did* want to do was to travel, be wildly successful, and have myself a grand old time doing it with a double martini in hand and expensive Italian sunglasses forever perched on my perfectly coiffed head. Needless to say, a family was not something that fit into that schema (not yet, at least), and back then the prospect of marrying someone was in my view tantamount to being incarcerated. It just was not something I considered; instead, I practically cringed at the thought of my freedom being compromised. I was forward-thinking, and I had dreams. It's not that I didn't want to have a family of my own someday, but turning into a housewife in the archaic and conventional Latina mold was to me like imposing failure on myself. It just wasn't in my cards. I needed more purpose, more glamour, more glitz, more fun, more adventures, *more . . .*

I finished my undergraduate degree at Loyola and then attended law school there, which would empower me with a whole new set of work ethic values. Law school really forced me to be an adult, demanding my total discipline and attention to ensure effective, quality studying that I could be proud of when all was said and done. I still managed to have all kinds of fun, but this new tier of academia meant it was also time to hanker down and get serious about my career.

After law school, in 1996 I returned to Puerto Rico. While I studied for the local and federal bar, I took a job on a TV variety game show as a host for a few months. It felt refreshing to take on a gig such as that, which was lighthearted and fun and a needed breath of fresh air as I worked hard to prepare for the law exams. Having hustled my way through high school and college, I was now poised to strut my stuff as a full-on career woman. I was back home, fueled with all kinds of new experiences, feeling more evolved and mature to take the next steps toward my future. I was finally going to be an attorney and was also able to work professionally as an actress-model. The last thing I expected in the television studio one afternoon was to catch the attention of one particular viewer, Jorge Posada. But he tells the story a bit differently . . .

PART II

Lessons in Love

I love you only because it's you the one I love.

—**PABLO NERUDA**

CHAPTER 5

Instinct and Serendipity

Jorge:

I don't know how else to say it, but from the moment I laid eyes on Laura, I knew deep down that if I played my cards right, she could very well become the greatest catch of my life. The first time I saw her (though she doesn't remember this) was actually ten whole years before I actually had the nerve to ask her out, but I do remember that first day vividly, as it played out on a sunny, grassy softball field on a hot day in Puerto Rico. Both of us were in high school, and I was umpiring a girls' softball game for a little extra cash. Laura, who regularly played in the league, was pitching for her team. I can still remember how she looked on that mound, utterly poised even at such a young age and clearly determined to play her heart out. She was an obvious leader but also a team player, balanced and calm but completely fierce when she needed to be. Totally enthralled, I found myself watching her every move.

For some reason her glove was broken, so, ever the gentleman, I offered her my own glove. This was my feeble attempt to show her that I was interested, to maybe send her some kind of little sign. She was so into her game, though, deep in the zone, focused on everything that was happening on the softball field—everything, that is, except for me. Clearly driven to compete at her best, she completely failed to pick up on the fact that I was even flirting with her via my glove gesture. I vividly remember her tremendous sense of concentration; but sadly, I just as vividly remember how quickly she blew me off. Her blatant indifference and quick dismissal left me to wonder about this beautiful and mysterious girl for the next decade. Though we exchanged only a few words that day, for those fleeting moments I was completely under her spell.

Laura still insists that she doesn't remember meeting me back then and claims that her first real encounter with me took place after she returned to Puerto Rico upon finishing law school at Loyola. One night, soon after her return, after I had seen her briefly on TV, we miraculously ended up at the same bar. Thankfully, Laura at least concedes to the notion of meeting me *that* night. Whose version of the story you decide to go with, you'd better believe that on the night of those drinks, I was convinced (again) that this woman would be the love of my life. The catch, of course, was to get her to believe the same thing. No easy task.

I made my move that night at Dunbar's when I saw her talking with Anita, a mutual friend, and went over to them with my heart in my throat.

"I want to meet your friend," I said.

"Oh, yeah?" Anita replied. "Get in line."

From the beginning she played hard to get, dismissing my advances with a wave of her hand or a roll of the eye, which, of course, only made me want to court her that much more. It seemed that nothing had changed since that ill-fated day on the softball field ten years earlier, when she had been just as uninterested in me as she seemed to be now. I didn't know exactly what it was about her, but for some reason I was fascinated and wanted to get to the bottom of why that was. This woman was nothing short of impossible, but there was something about her that also told me to stay the course. I knew I needed to trust my gut on this one, despite the seemingly terrible odds.

I would call our friend Anita every single day, pleading that she somehow try to convince Laura to budge. "Listen," she would implore Laura, "Jorge really wants to hang out." But Laura kept blowing me off, saying she had a boyfriend and that she was not interested. That was November.

In December, Laura and said boyfriend apparently broke up. Around that time, Anita invited her to come out with a group of us for a night of bowling. Maybe she was feeling a bit down on the heels of her breakup, or maybe she just needed to get out of the house. Whatever the reason, I was delighted to finally have a chance to talk to her and grateful that Anita had at last made it happen. The group went to pick her up—with me sitting cheerfully at the wheel of the Ford Expedition in eager anticipation. Four other people were sitting in the back, so the passenger seat was conveniently empty for her.

"You don't remember me," I said, "but we met ten years ago when you were pitching a softball game. I lent you my glove, you were number ten, your uniform was black, white, and yellow . . . and you wore gray socks." By the look of shock on her face, she might very well have been thinking "psycho alert," clearly unable to wrap her head around the fact that I could remember and register every detail of her outfit from ten years before, never mind recall her number. That night while we bowled I interrogated her, question after question, like some kind of personal interview. I asked her if she wanted to ever get married, how many kids she wanted to have, what kind of food she liked to cook, what her favorite color was, what places she had traveled to, what her goals were, what languages she spoke, if she was a morning person, if she was a vegetarian, a righty or a lefty, if she slept with one or two pillows, what kind of pillows, and on and on and on. I wanted to know everything about her. I was on a mission, but again, despite my perseverance, she didn't pay too much attention and treated me—no more, no less—like every other person in the bar.

Derek Jeter (fellow New York Yankee):

I remember Jorge calling me from Puerto Rico and talking up this amazing girl he had met, bragging about her, and desperately wanting to ask her out. When I came to visit him one off-season, we drove all over the island on a frantic hunt for this girl, and as it turned out, one night out at a bar, we actually saw her. Can you imagine that after weeks in her pursuit, Laura walked right past him, *and he didn't even say a word?* He was completely intimidated by her, which of course I thought was totally hysterical. And I ended up spending the rest of my trip in Puerto Rico helping Jorge find this mystery woman again, hoping this time that he would make me proud and at least have the courage to say hello.

I went home feeling completely defeated. I figured that I had blown my chance, but, despite the blatant rejection, I continued to call her, trusting my initial instincts that the essence of this woman was a reason to persist.

During the off-season, I would lie on my couch with the phone on my belly, literally waiting to see if Laura would call. My friends would ask what the hell I was doing, and I'd respond by complaining about the fact that she never called. I remember even asking them if something was wrong with the phone. She *never* called me back, she never picked up the phone when I called, and the few times she did pick up, she always managed to blow me off somehow. My friends thought I was out of my mind; they had never seen me act this way over any woman and probably found the whole thing wildly funny. But this crush of mine was bigger than I was, and I don't think all the male mockery in the world could have stopped it.

At the risk of being a total sucker, I persisted. One day I phoned her, as I routinely did, and though I'd gotten accustomed to her complete indifference to me, that particular day, for some reason, she actually bit back. I don't know what it was that I said or did differently during that call that made her budge, but finally she seemed to be letting her guard down. At first she defiantly said that she was busy every single night, and then ultimately (for reasons unknown to me) she let up a bit and proceeded to ask me if I played racquetball.

"Interesting," I thought, "a sports date." Of course that made me even more excited about our phone call and the plans that I hoped we were about to cook up. Things were looking brighter by the moment. I told her that I did play, and she told me to meet her at the racquetball court at a certain hour the next day. She didn't ask me what I wanted to do or even how I was doing. She was all business, which instead of putting me off only excited me more. I believed she fully intended to kick my ass to the point of such utter humiliation that I would finally stop hounding her. However, about an hour before we were supposed to meet she received an unexpected casting call for a television commercial, because at the time she was going on auditions for modeling and acting jobs in addition to studying for her exams. At least she gave me the courtesy of showing up at the racquetball court; but when she arrived all frantic and frazzled she said, "Listen, I have a casting today. If you want to come with me, fantastic, and we can play after. If not, sorry, man, but this is your chance. Take it or leave it." The look on her face told me she was dead serious—this really was going to be my chance, and, racquetball or not, I was determined not to waste it. I could tell Laura was serious about her work, and though we had made a date just one day before, I knew very well that I hadn't yet registered as too high a priority for her.

I agreed to the whole plan and went right along to the casting, quietly sitting there in her shadow and relishing it the whole time. Instead of feeling bad because our first and long-overdue date was being postponed, I felt lucky to be a fly on the wall, watching Laura in all her splendor do her best to convince the casting people in question that she was the woman for their spot. She was vivacious, funny, present, and strong in her audition, which only told me more about just how dynamic she really was. I was actually happy the date had unfolded this way and even took it as a compliment that she would even think to take me along. After all, she had never shown any qualms in dodging me before, so why would I have thought that this was going to be any different? But here I finally was, and I was thrilled; I was getting to know more facets of this alluring female who for reasons I can't explain had me acting like a schoolboy.

After her appointment we went straight to the racquetball court, where we would play for several hours and where I would see yet another side of Laura—her physical prowess and ability to compete. She was a total warrior, showing dexterity, grace, and strength throughout the whole match. However, while we were playing I accidentally slammed the little ball right into her butt, which left a nasty bruise on her for about two weeks. Looking back, I like to believe it was meant to be a reminder, so that she wouldn't forget me—an impression, if you will. After we played, I asked her what she was doing that night, to which she quickly and adamantly replied that she would be staying home. Though she resisted, I was intuitive enough to pick up on the fact that she had actually had fun throughout our little encounter. At least I knew she did not hate me, and I would even go as far as to say that I detected some mild flirtation on the court. "You're not staying home," I countered. "I'm coming back to pick you up in half an hour." I sensed that the tables were starting to turn, and I was definitely not going to let her get away.

That night we went out for cocktails and had a fantastic time. I don't know what changed, but it was clear that something had shifted, because from one day to the next I felt that my interest in this impossible woman was at last starting to be reciprocated. I didn't want to get ahead of myself, but I began to notice a slight twinkle in her eye when she spoke to me and even the hint of a coy little smile when I spoke to her. What had once been a definite "no way" on her part now seemed to be morphing into a "well . . . why not?" Her sudden change of heart only heightened whatever feelings I had worked up for her over the years. Moving forward, I was intent on playing my cards right. This was it.

But after that night out, there was no denying it: the romance radar was clearly starting to flash red, and the chemistry was now starting to crackle mutually. A few days later, I left an Alejandro Fernández CD in her mailbox; then another day I left a note on her car saying "Have a great day," which she discovered after leaving the courtroom that afternoon. What can I say? "Utterly smitten" would be an understatement to describe how I now felt about Laura. Here was a girl who had it all: brains, beauty, and a heart of gold. Plus, I got a tremendous kick out of her. She made me laugh to no end, and seeing her smile always gave me a feeling of completeness. She navigated her life with equal parts class, fun, and a sense of personal accomplishment that always inspired me. I saw her as an all-around superwoman and felt that every moment spent with her could teach me something—or at the very least thoroughly entertain me.

The heat was turning up, but she knew that I was going to have to leave at the start of the season, and perhaps to protect herself, she tried to simmer things down. I can't blame her: though she was starting to like me, she knew full well about

Tino Martinez (fellow New York Yankee): ─────────

> Once Jorge started dating Laura, she was all he could
> talk about. It was clear he was taken with her. I think he
> was the most serious he ever felt about a woman, and
> he never talked about another girl again. She clearly
> made an impact.

the general reputation of baseball players—as womanizers and
cheaters—and didn't want to find herself in a relationship with
someone who was always traveling, someone whom she would
always have to wonder about. I did my best to make sure she
knew that she would never have to wonder about me, because
to the degree that I have ever known anything serious about
myself, I knew that I was in love with her from day one.

One night around this time, in every possible manner
known to me, I tried to convince Laura to be my girl. I imagined
that a woman like her was highly sought after, and I didn't want
to take any risks while I was away. I wanted to know that she
was as committed as I was, and I swallowed every last bit of my
pride to express this. She kept resisting (again, probably in self-
protection), and when I took her home, sitting there in the car in
front of her house, we said an overly dramatic good-bye, as if we
would never see each other again. "At the very least you can give
me a kiss," I finally mustered the nerve to say (in my defense, it
had already been like four months and not even *one* kiss). She

finally gave me the long-overdue kiss, and it felt as though the entire world literally stopped moving for that moment.

She left the car, rolled down the window, and said, "I'll see you tomorrow."

It felt great to know that all of my hard work had finally paid off and even more that I had not totally hallucinated the chemistry between us. It was real, and now she could resist until she was blue in the face—but I could tell from that kiss that she did in fact like me. From that point on, we started to really spend time together.

For the next several weeks, there were lots of adorable gestures and outward reminders, and before we knew it we were completely and mutually in love. One night she invited me to come for dinner, and she made white rice, black beans, and stuffed filet. She told me early on, "I don't clean, I don't do laundry, I don't iron, and I don't plan on learning. The only thing I do is cook, so you better be okay with that." Fortunately for both of us, I was more than okay, and from the moment I tasted the food she served me, I knew I would marry her.

CHAPTER 6

Lessons in Perseverance and Surprises

Laura:

You have to understand that before I met Jorge, I was the kind of girl who blazed with confidence, especially as far as men were concerned. I was lucky enough to have always had boyfriends, and I was the kind of girl who didn't make a big fuss about my own love interests and crushes. It was as if I knew the boys would come and go and I would rather spend my energy on staying focused and ambitious. On Friday afternoons through-out my teens and twenties, the phone would ring consistently. I was never at a loss for plans or company, and I was happy to play the social butterfly. I liked to be friends with everyone instead of being part of just one group and made it a point to always leave my options open. I reveled in my role as the gregarious little diva, and for many years I considered that a serious boyfriend of any kind would ultimately be a burden.

In Loyola, I'd strut to class as if I were on some kind of fashion catwalk, walking as if the wind were created especially to blow my hair in just the right way. So by the time I was back in Puerto Rico, fully dating Jorge, the poor man still had the ungodly task of trying to tame me. My daily routine at the time was nothing short of insane. Each morning, I would leave the house with three different bags packed and ready: the office bag, the gym bag, and the one for going on auditions. At any point I could be carrying an arsenal of makeup, a racquetball racquet, sneakers, high heels, a sports bra, hosiery, and a brief-case full of paperwork. From briefings and trainings to photo shoots and rehearsals, I wore three different hats, juggling and hustling as I always knew how. My life as a lawyer was serious and focused, so modeling and acting balanced me with a sense of fun. Both of those activities certainly require a person to stay in shape, so the training element was always a must. In general, it was a dynamic time when I literally felt as though I could *and would* do it all. The world was my oyster, and I was not afraid to dive in. Though I was incredibly happy with Jorge as my man, I knew that I would never compromise my own professional and personal agendas as a relentlessly ambitious person. I had things to accomplish, lessons to learn, success to prove, adventures to embark upon—and no relationship was going to turn the volume down on any of those goals.

In October, Jorge was to play in the World Series, after a season when the Yankees steamrolled to a 125–50 record and a four-game sweep of the Padres. So, I decided it wouldn't be the end of the world if I took off for a holiday in Mexico with some friends. I guess there was still a part of me that was afraid to completely release the last shreds of my freedom, and maybe this tropical jaunt was my way of showing him (and myself) that I could still do what I wanted. Being a typical Latin male, he completely flipped out, imagining me gallivanting all through Mexico in a string bikini, frosty margaritas in my hand. I guess he figured he needed to take some radical action, because one night after I returned from my Mexican getaway, we were out for dinner and he suggested we share a piece of cheesecake after the meal. I had never really been a dessert girl, but the dinner had been so perfect that something sweet was definitely in order. When the waiter brought us the confection, glistening on top of the creamy white crown of the classic dessert was an engagement ring. My entire future was on that cheesecake.

My sense of independence flashed before my eyes, and I realized that accepting Jorge would mean I would be tied down, spoken for, not free—all the things I feared the most. This really was the moment of truth. Before me was a man who was willing to do anything for me, who had chased me relentlessly without flinching once, a man whom I knew would unconditionally love me forever. At the end of the day, *didn't I want just that?* Was this not as important as anything else I had on my list of musts?

Though I had always regarded myself as ambitious and modern, I
still could not deny my roots, which were grounded by a sense of
family that I am sure made me who I am. Yes, I'd always wanted
lots of things—but I could not deny that somewhere deep inside,
I also wanted to truly love and be loved. I had to think this one
through carefully. I felt the potency of the moment in my heartbeat, feeling it deep within, where my instincts reside. No matter
how much I resisted, I could not escape it any longer: Jorge was
indeed the one for me. At last, I began to allow myself to accept
the blessing of this relationship and the prospect of our beautiful
future together.

The whole restaurant was looking at us, and it dawned
on me that if I said "no" right now, I would never be able to
come back and say "yes." But for whatever reason my instinct
was instead to punch him in the shoulder. But he knew me well
enough by now to know that my strike was just a nervous reaction, so he took a deep breath and proceeded to ask me a second
time. I had to take a few deep breaths myself, knowing that it was
time to make a decision. I could not skirt around the issue any
longer. This time, I answered, "Yes, but on one condition"—the
lawyer in me had to insert a clause—"we wait one whole year
before we get married." This seemed like a perfect solution to
my quandary: on the one hand, I would pledge my commitment
in the form of our engagement, but I would give myself a year
to digest and process the whole thing. Fair is fair, I thought. Jorge
agreed; after all, he just wanted to be sure that I wouldn't really

Manuel Mendez (Laura's brother):

> Of course when Laura told us she was dating a
> ballplayer, all of us wondered what kind of guy he
> would be. You know how it is with celebrity athletes,
> they're all over the news, and this was my little sister we
> were dealing with. But it was always so clear that Jorge
> only had eyes for Laura. He really gave me the sense
> that he would always take care of her. As her brother, I
> instantly felt that she would always be safe with him.

go anywhere, what with my Mexico escapade looming in his
imagination like a recurring nightmare.

By now everyone in the restaurant was clapping and cheer-
ing, and all I could see before me was the massive smile on
my new fiancé's face. I could feel his excitement (and probably
relief), and honestly, I was just as happy. After that quick moment
of fear, the joy kicked in and I allowed myself to get excited
about what the rest of my life would look like.

Shortly after his proposal, Jorge bought his first house and I
helped him get it up and running. We were now officially engaged,
and this would be our first home together. One day at a time, I
slowly allowed myself to grasp the reality of the changing pan-
orama, simultaneously letting myself fall deeper in love. My fears
of losing my independence were now gradually being tempered
by the relief of knowing that I would always be in excellent hands,

endlessly loved by a good man with a beautiful heart. I could feel myself growing up as a woman, at last starting to redirect my energies and efforts outward, beyond just myself. We were a team now. And just like that, I gave myself permission to soften.

By the summer of 1998, although we were engaged, I started to put the wheels into motion for another longtime fantasy—a backpacking trip through Europe with my friend Roxanna. Needless to say, Jorge was not keen on this latest endeavor of mine, but I was steadfast, and no one, not even Jorge, was going to keep me from the potentially magical journey that lay ahead. I had done the fancy-pants Europe thing with my parents as a kid, seeing the interior of every church in every town, and now I wanted to see Europe my way, through my own grown-up eyes. I got myself a backpack, a Eurail pass, and maps for every city. Perhaps I knew that life after marriage would not allow for such spontaneity and wanted to milk the last phase of my independence to the last drop. Europe seemed like the perfect place to wander with a close friend. I imagined myself sipping fancy teas in London and buying leather boots in Italy. I envisioned our post-trip scrapbooks already, loaded with photos of Roxanna and me with our massive backpacks strapped on and smiles on our faces from here to Milan. Our agenda would include long, lingering afternoons sitting leisurely in cafés, baguettes with butter, pizza napoletana, green parks with splendid floral landscapes, and the chance to bond as buddies over the magic of it all. As far as Roxanna and I were concerned, this was going to be the most epic adventure of our lives.

You know that saying "We make plans and God laughs"? Well, God must have been downright cracking up when a few weeks before the big trip, on an eerily dark and stormy day, after four pregnancy tests, assured confirmation from my doctor, and much inner turmoil—I found out that I was carrying my first child. I was standing in front of the bathroom mirror when they first called me from the doctor's office, and in that moment the house became a shade darker, with me standing at the center of this mysterious gloom in total disbelief. The notion of having a baby was to me synonymous to being tied down. It was one thing that I was engaged to Jorge; that was something I could handle and wrap my head around. But being pregnant meant the end of my life as I knew it and the beginning of an entirely different part of my life that I knew I would want one day—just not yet.

It meant giving up my freedom, which was the complete opposite of what I had in mind. My bags were already packed for Europe, I had managed to get Jorge to give me his blessing, our engagement was on, and all the pieces had been lined up perfectly. This pregnancy would change everything. I still felt I had so much to do, wild oats to sow, memories to make, and adventures to embark upon. That year was supposedly going to give me time to think about marriage and really determine if it was what I wanted.

I knew that we were both athletes, that we both wanted always to be winners, that we wanted a lot of the same things, and that we had a good time together—but I was certainly not ready to mother Jorge's children. Honestly, I had to keep myself from not punching *myself* in the belly this time. When I got off the phone with the doctor, I dropped to the ground and started to cry. Not only was it the most unexpected piece of news that we could possibly receive, but it also definitely meant that my trip to Europe would be shot. And though Jorge and I were very much in love, we were young, and the prospect of a family was not something we were necessarily ready to contend with.

"Are you sitting down?" I asked Jorge after I was able to collect myself and call him to give him the news. "If you're not, you better sit down, because what I am about to tell you is completely crazy—you're going to be a dad." He was clearly stunned and caught completely off guard, but I could also hear the excitement in his voice. He wanted to start telling all his friends. He was significantly calmer than I was, but maybe he was just holding himself together to show strength and optimism at a moment that seemed to hang precariously in the air. Now that I was pregnant, we were collectively thrown into it: there would be no waiting and also no turning back.

My father, surprisingly enough, took the news better than my mother. I remember sitting with her one day for lunch and asking, "Who would you rather be pregnant? Me or Letty [my brother's wife]?" My mom, of course, said "Letty," because of the two of us, Letty was the one who was already married. "Too bad," I told her, "it's me." She gently put her fork down, and I could sense that a lump was starting to form in her throat. Her face went white and her eyes wide. There was an empty silence between us for what seemed like half an hour, the air thick with the unforeseeable news that I'd just delivered in what I now realize was too casual a manner. She looked at me as if I had just dropped an unspeakable bomb. Like my father, she'd always had high hopes for me, and she probably believed that an accidental pregnancy might throw a major wrench into what she'd imagined was going to be a perfect, smooth-sailing life. She always wanted things to be done right, by the book, with a high regard for a traditional sense of morality, which she herself never questioned. My siblings and I were raised with these values, and the thought of these core moral ideals being compromised in any way likely mortified her. I knew she was not going to take it well, but I decided that I would be better served by telling her right away and getting her on board as a supporter and friend. I also knew that once the initial shock wore off, she would start to simmer down and eventually accept the idea that things don't always happen the way we expect them to.

"You know you're going to have to tell your father," she said. Maybe her reaction was just a forewarning of what she believed my dad would have to say. However, when I did tell him he just looked up at me from the couch in the living room and, totally poker-faced, said, "Okay." If I had to guess, I'd say he knew deep down that Jorge and I would do the right thing and follow through with our engagement. He knew how he had raised me and was confident that we were going to be as responsible about this as we could. I was grateful for his silent assurance and knew that in time my mom would come around too.

The alternatives swirled in my mind, but somewhere deep down I realized that the only choice I really had was to face the music. After the initial shock, after the moment of bleak uncertainty, some inner instinct told me that I had to have this baby. Something inside me clicked, saying that it was time to grow up. Everything that seemed "important" in my life flashed quickly into my mind, and as much as I tried to fight it, I could not deny that *family* was somewhere at the top of that list. So it had come sooner than I'd planned, but now that it was here, I needed to take accountability for it.

Now pregnant, I also realized that I was going to have to have a relationship with the baby's father for the rest of my life, for better or worse. I thought: I've been totally selfish my whole life, I've done everything for myself, and now I have this great guy who loves me to death, who vows to always be with me and give me everything. We had just bought a house, and we really were crazy in love. I didn't have to look too closely to see that everything was in place and lined up for that baby to come into the world. I knew by now that I could not imagine my life without Jorge, and, as I said, deep down I also knew that I would one day want a family just like the one I had been lucky enough to grow up in. Maybe this was it, the one chance you get to create something meaningful and beautiful; the divine opportunity to begin the creation of my own family. I somehow knew that I shouldn't ignore this primordial pull. Maybe Europe was not meant to happen for a reason? I can change, I thought. I'll stop drinking, smoking, and partying. Women do it all the time. Maybe this was my time. I started to think that I could be a mom, just like all the other moms I knew. After all, I'd had a babysitter growing up and I'd turned out okay; Jorge and I could have the baby, hire a babysitter, and continue my old plan as if nothing had happened. How hard could it really be? Little did I know that the road ahead of us would bring all kinds of surprises—the kind you cannot plan or prepare for and that demand your total presence at every moment. My pregnancy would essentially redirect the course of my life, and in ways I could have never expected. As assertive and focused as I had always been until now, nothing could have prepared me for what would come with this baby.

CHAPTER 7

On the Precipice of Success

Jorge:

I was only twenty-eight years old when Laura found out she was pregnant, and though I can't deny the fact that I mildly panicked, I mostly received the news as a beautiful blessing, something to accept with gratitude and joy. I guess I felt that way because for as long as I can remember I have always wanted to have kids. Whenever I pictured my future, a wife and kids were at the center of it. My own roots had been strong, and I knew that part of my job in this life was to make them even deeper by creating a family of my own. Along with baseball, family was one of the things that defined me, so when Laura told me that she was pregnant, yes, I was caught off guard—but totally and unquestionably exhilarated nonetheless.

Although Laura was clearly worried, I was more on the excited side and sort of felt that it was all happening this way for a reason. I wanted to believe that the unexpected pregnancy meant it was our duty, as a couple in love, to step up and start our family. The universe works in mysterious ways, so I tried to understand this latest twist as something that was meant to happen, perhaps for reasons that were not so clear. I chose to have faith at a time that could have easily been perceived as a crisis. Though Laura was having a difficult time accepting it with as much optimism as I had, I worked really hard to convince her that everything was going to be okay.

My career too was really starting to take off, and 1998 was a real turning point for me. Things were definitely getting hot for the team, and it was beyond thrilling to be able to be a part of it. I was playing baseball for the greatest team in the world and partaking of some truly magical moments out there on the field. It all felt so fast, everything happening at the same time, the momentum riding on itself as we prepared for what would be a life in New York as newlyweds and parents.

Laura packed up, quit her job as an attorney, stopped taking modeling and acting gigs, and decided that she would also relocate to Manhattan for the season. Her plan was to study to take the New York State bar so that she could also practice law in the United States. She was very clear about the fact that she did not simply want to be an overprivileged "baseball wife," and she needed some kind of strategy of her own in New York. She was intent on staying busy, active, and fully engaged in every detail of our new life in the city.

Along with the move to New York and the developing pregnancy, the other issue on the table was our wedding. There was no question: it was time to tie the knot, and our plan was to do it in New York. We gave it some thought and came to the conclusion that with Laura pregnant, we would be best off doing something low-key and quick. We decided to do something fast and small there, with the intention of later throwing a more elaborate affair with our friends and family in Puerto Rico. Because of the pregnancy we had to change the date for our real wedding anyway, and I was playing at the time so I didn't have the luxury of taking any more time off. We wanted to be practical about it by getting it done quickly and quietly for the time being.

But Laura was not going to go down without a fight, and she managed to pull all kinds of shenanigans before we would actually get to say our "I dos."

I'll never forget the morning we went to pick up our marriage documents from City Hall. There was a revolving glass door at the entrance, and instead of walking through it normally and entering the building, Laura—ever the comedienne—lingered within the door and followed it back out into the street, where she stood with a grin from ear to ear, looking at me like a true prankster who'd just gotten away with a heist. She waved at me as if she were waving to someone she had just seen at the mall, knowing full well that her little game was just her way of stalling. I stood inside the building, laughing hysterically at her antics, and waved for her to come inside. After her little scene, we finally managed to pick up the papers and were now ready for the ceremony.

Roberto Clemente, Jr., the famous ballplayer (and the son of my longtime hero), who was also our friend, told us he had a great minister who could marry us right in our home in Manhattan. I had a game on the day of our wedding, so Laura waited for me at home, getting herself ready (inside and out) for our big day. From the moment she woke up that day, she was a complete mess. Maybe it was the pregnancy hormones, the reality of the fact that we were about to get married, or a gnarly combination of both—but she was in distress and there was not much I could do about it. I just kept hoping that she would somehow snap out of it and come around, but I can also appreciate how surreal the moment must have been for my pregnant bride-to-be, who was about to tie the knot during a four-person ceremony in a small New York apartment.

After the game, I scrambled home as fast as I could, only to find my poor bride in prewedding shambles. She was clearly scared, perhaps working through the fact that she was about to become somebody's wife and not having an easy time digesting it. She wanted to travel the world and have fun, and this moment meant that all of that might be suddenly compromised. The wedding only reinforced her initial fears that had come up when she found out about the pregnancy, maybe sealing the deal in a way that felt too close, too real. I understood her completely and more than anything just wanted to help her get through it. I knew that she wanted to be there, but I also knew that this might not have been how she had always imagined her wedding day would be.

I thought it would be a good idea to distract her a bit and decided to take her out for some pizza while we waited for Roberto Clemente, Jr.'s, "minister" to arrive. There we were, eating a slice of New York City pizza as if it were any other day in the world, while our wedding day was on the brink of becoming totally real. The distraction seemed to help a little, but I could see that her heart was racing and her mind was somewhere else. I kept giving her a pep talk, assuring her that everything would be fine, that she would still be the same Laura she had always been, and that I was the happiest man on the planet for getting to share my life with her.

While we were out, Laura's sister called, screaming that the minister had arrived. We returned home, with the adrenaline gradually starting to rise, and poor Laura went straight to our bedroom. I prayed that she would keep her pizza down and that in time she would be okay and we could just get on with it. But I could tangibly feel her nerves and wanted to respect whatever time and space she needed before we went on. She knew she was at the edge of a major cliff, and the concept of taking the proverbial leap toward domesticity just mortified her.

It's not that she didn't love me; I never doubted that. But she had always been a strong, independent girl with big dreams, and I know the idea of marriage threatened some of her youthful fantasies. Of course, none of that ever really bugged me—because I always knew that we belonged together. After much coercing and patience, we finally got her out of the bathroom and could at last carry on with the ceremony.

The minister, wearing a ruffled shirt and polyester suit and with a full-fledged Afro, was there waiting for us, along with our only two guests, Laura's sister, who was the maid of honor; and my colleague Derek Jeter, who was the best man. I think Laura was a bit stunned by the whole thing. She probably imagined that she was supposed to be somewhere in Europe, maybe hiking an extreme trail somewhere in the Swiss Alps, enjoying a fresh prosciutto panino in Florence, or shopping like a character out of *Sex and the City* in Paris—but instead, here she was about to be married to a New York Yankees baseball player by a minister with an Afro in a polyester suit. We stood in the living room of our newly rented apartment, and the minister began to speak.

"I know a lot of people get married and it doesn't end up meaning anything," he said. "But I was married for many years, and sadly my wife passed away. And I didn't realize how much I loved her until I lost her. So if you two love each other, I encourage you to milk every moment that you have together, because each one is precious, and you never know what life may bring." I could tell his words struck both of us, and in that moment realized that God was indeed bestowing upon us a gift, one of those blessings that doesn't come around too often. Maybe the special quality of this moment meant something deeper than we could imagine. It was indeed finally time to grow up and be real, and I could see that Laura was also feeling the weight of the minister's words.

The minister asked for the rings, and, well, we didn't even have any rings. We were so utterly unprepared and had not really thought any of it through. We just wanted to get married and call it a day—all of the formalities would have to be dealt with later. So we went ahead and did it without the rings, and officially became Mr. and Mrs. Jorge Posada on that beautiful April afternoon.

After the makeshift New York wedding, we gradually started to settle into our new life. Laura sailed smoothly through the pregnancy and was really enjoying life in the city. She seemed to be getting used to the idea of becoming a mom and even starting to enjoy it. By now I was beyond excited too, especially when we found out that we would be having a little boy. Being a baseball player and all, you can imagine the fantasies I was starting to entertain about the whole father-son thing. I thought back to the early days with my dad and definitely looked forward to getting to re-create some of those moments with my own boy. I envisioned it all—playing catch, riding bikes, having the chance to teach him about sports and sportsmanship, and generally being able to witness a little person come into his own under our care and guidance. With each day that passed and every millimeter that my wife's belly grew, I became more and more excited about the future of our family.

Laura began the coordinating for our real wedding in Puerto Rico, which we decided would take place in January 2000. She dived right into planning mode, choosing invitations, colors, menus, photographer—the whole nine yards. I was happy to see her busy and consumed and was grateful that by now her nerves had calmed down and she seemed to really be enjoying the pace of our life. She was excited about getting to actualize the wedding she had always dreamed of, with all our friends and family present in a collective celebration of our love. I wanted her to have that, and honestly, I wanted it just as badly, too.

Now that Laura's anxieties were less present, I could start to see the genuine excitement in her attitude, which of course only heightened my own.

By now I was also playing a lot more as the everyday catcher for the team, and I made the All-Star Game for the first time. My career had taken on a life of its own, and, coupled with the ridiculously exciting fact that my firstborn son was due in November, my life seemed to be moving in a wonderful direction. It felt as though everything I had ever worked for, as an athlete and as a man, was now coming into full fruition. The skies were open for me, it seemed, and my outlook could not have been more positive.

CHAPTER 8

Living the Dream

Laura:

Everything seemed to be falling right into place. I was start-ing to adjust to married life, frankly because New York was such an exciting place to be. Before we arrived there, I was sure that I had seen it all as a college student in New Orleans, almost cocky about the fact that I had already lived in a major U.S. city. But Manhattan would school me in the art of urban living and the thrill of participating in the cultural experience that defines life in such a dynamic place. I instantly adored the rhythm of the city, its steady and electrifying pulse, and the nonstop stimulation that came with every day. Simply getting from point A to point B in New York could be nothing short of a mini-adventure, each face on the street having some story to tell about its roots and every block showing a distinct personality of its own. From fine dining and shopping to shows, art galleries, and parks, I found myself exhilarated on a daily basis. Being in such a glorious place, pregnant with my first child and on the brink of soon having our real wedding in Puerto Rico, felt like total perfection.

Jorge was amazed at my ability to slip into the pace of things, and it was evident that we were now jointly excited about the chapter that lay ahead. It was just the two of us, so there was a special vacation quality to those months, as I spent my days sorting out our apartment and planning for what would be our "real" wedding in Puerto Rico. I created a daily routine for myself that would ensure that each day had purpose and all the while tried to sync up with the energetic hustle of the city. I shopped for furniture, I decorated, and I diligently went to the gym each day with my growing belly in tow. Exercise was a way for me to center myself, and whether I was in New Orleans, Puerto Rico, New York, or anywhere else in the world, I would always try to stick to my regimen. It has constantly been a way for me to center myself, which was something I needed desperately when we first arrived in New York. Especially now that I was pregnant, I was intent on staying as healthy and fit as possible. Not to mention the fact that I wanted to look beautiful for my "real" wedding in Puerto Rico.

Luckily, Manhattan felt like my playground, distracting me from the reality that I had recently become someone's wife. Instead, in New York I found myself reveling in my role as Jorge's partner, proud to be on his arm and genuinely delighted about everything that was about to come. By now we had both accepted my pregnancy as a blessing, and, despite the initial shock, we couldn't have been happier about the prospect of starting our family. I had gone through my moment of panic, I had already thrown my little fit—but now I found myself as ready as ever to walk down this road with Jorge by my side.

It was an exciting time for so many reasons. Besides all the wedding fever and pregnancy bliss, I was also starting to get more personally involved in Jorge's career. The Yankees were definitely on the rise, and he had not been very happy with his agents, so I started to take more of a role in his representation. I would attend his meetings and review all of his documents, trying to get my head around each situation so that I could best assess and advise. I had always been immensely proud of my husband, and being this close to his career dealings now gave me an even more profound appreciation of his accomplishments. Working by his side reminded me daily of the reasons that I had fallen for him in the first place and gave me another sense of purpose that made our partnership that much more solid. We were in it together on every level. Not only did this add a whole new dimension to our relationship, but I was also now finally realizing my lifelong dream of working in sports or entertainment law. Our worlds were starting to gel all around, and the synergy of our union as a couple was really taking shape. We never fought, we were always happy, and so many positive things seemed to be happening at once. It became very easy for me to picture our future, laden with all the triumphs of our combined successes, all of it under-scored by our mutual desire to prevail as winners. Those fanciful scenes would continue to unfold in my mind as I engaged the energy of our current sense of achievement to fantasize about what tomorrow would look like—and from where we were standing back then, tomorrow looked pretty damn good.

The team road-tripped a lot, and I gladly joined them. It was such a unique treat to be able to partake of what seemed like perfect camaraderie to me. When I look back on it now, I remember it as a montage of deliriously happy moments shared by a group of people who genuinely enjoyed one another's company. I remember hanging out with all the Latin players, such as Bernie Williams, Tino Martinez, Luis Sojo, El Duque Hernandez, Mariano Rivera, and Ramiro Mendoza, and all of their wives were also around, so there was this terrific aura of solidarity and we were all very close. The fact that we were spending a lot of our time with fellow Hispanics made every moment feel close to home, which of course helped to further ease me into my new environment. Away from Puerto Rico, our daily life with those people would amp us with a sense of community, the kind of closeness that we were accustomed to and had grown up with.

New York City was already the most exciting place in the world, so the chance to share it with our new friends felt like some kind of magical privilege. We would sit at the games together, and there was always a healthy dose of laughter and togetherness. Everyone seemed to get along famously, and there was an amazing vibration among the team, on and off the field.

We would dine together at many of the city's spectacular restaurants, hitting the scene like a bunch of giddy children with what felt like a constant desire to celebrate. Everyone was young and energetic, and though I was pregnant and tired a lot of the time, I remember feeling that those months in the city would become some of my most memorable ever. There was never a dull moment, and every weekend brought with it some new and thrilling adventure—be it a road trip with the guys or an amazing group brunch that would last for hours. I could begin to feel the wonder of what it meant to be part of a group like the Yankees, an energy that somehow felt contagious when you were among the players. It was inspiring to see them all together not only as colleagues but also as friends and brothers who seemed to adore one another without conditions. I felt lucky to be able to witness those connections and excited about further cultivating relationships with my new friends.

The team felt strong, with a magical sense of morale and a very special energy in the air that you could actually feel. I attended as many games as I could, highly charged gatherings that brought together the spirit of sportsmanship, old-school athletic sensibilities, and all kinds of fun. It was an absolute blast to hold court with such amazing and talented people, who as individuals were amazing but who as a group radiated with the unique collective force of people who were happy, hopeful, and exhilarated all at once. We were collectively optimistic, and there was a general feeling of being unstoppable.

I will never forget one particular autumn afternoon in New York, when, after another Yankees World Series win, for the first time I got to ride along with Jorge in the celebratory ticker-tape parade from Broadway down through to City Hall Park, in all of my newlywed and pregnant glory, as all of New York City watched in delight. The colors of the changing leaves looked extra pretty to me that day, and the sky seemed bluer and crisper than ever. The temperature of the air felt perfect, and the joy on my husband's face was as evident as my own. The moment felt charged with possibility, pointing us both toward what seemed like an amazing future. Our courtship had taken me from my home in Puerto Rico to the center of New York, and now every detail of my life seemed to be part of some larger plan that I could only begin to intuit. I fancied myself the luckiest woman in the world, blessed by some divine providence and happy to cruise forward on the crest of our mutual momentum.

PART III

Tough Love

We cannot learn without pain.

—ARISTOTLE

CHAPTER 9

A New Reality
Is Born

Jorge:

The universe has a funny way of creating vicissitudes. One minute you are the picture of accomplishment and glamour, riding around with your spirits up and your hopes high, fancying yourself one of the lucky ones, determined to entertain a jubilant life, sure of yourself, of your behavior and your decisions. But in less than a split second, before you can even turn around to give a wave of gratitude to your loved ones and adoring fans, the universe reminds you, in her ever-mysterious way, of your fundamental, unarguable mortality. As for us, we certainly did not realize on that crisp autumn day during the celebratory parade down Fifth Avenue in Manhattan, as we were cheered on by millions of zealous Yankees fans and proud New Yorkers, ticker tape raining on us like a magical snowfall, that this reign of glory of ours was on the brink of a dark and stormy chaos.

On November 28, 1999, our first child, Jorge L. Posada, Jr., was born in San Juan, Puerto Rico, where we returned after the Yankees won the World Series against the Atlanta Braves, excited to have the birth in our own hometown, together with our family and friends, who were all waiting with joy and anticipation. Much like expectant parents everywhere, we were eager to meet our son and to begin the exciting journey of parenthood, which we had always seen as the grand and beautiful culmination of our love as a couple. We were ready for that world of interminable cuteness that we always imagined would come with the birth of a baby, everything cast in pastels and softness. We were ready for adorable fuzzy presents and joyful relatives, and smiles and hugs and laughter all around. We were even ready for that crazy-sounding baby language that adults use to communicate with infants. We wanted it all, knowing that we were at a point in our lives where we would be able to provide for a family adequately and fuel that family with all kinds of love.

By the end of the month, after all of the excitement and commotion, Laura was ready to pop. She felt haggard, swollen, and tired but was nevertheless ecstatic at the prospect of our new baby. Finally, on the twenty-eighth day of the month, when the temperature in the air was just slightly starting to change, we were at home resting, when all of a sudden Laura shot up, ran to the toilet, and screamed when no urine came out. Instead, a flood of water came gushing out of her like a fountain. She howled like a madwoman, which of course got my attention, and within seconds I was with her in the bathroom, trying to calm her down.

Despite being completely and utterly hysterical, the woman wanted to *take a shower*. Can you imagine? She was crashed out on the floor, amniotic fluid flowing out of her like the Rio Grande, screaming at the top of her lungs, and she still wanted to take her shower! Somehow or other she managed to do so, and in the interim I got our things packed and ready, called the hospital to make arrangements, and of course notified both of our parents. It was clearly showtime, and although things were starting to feel hectic, I was beyond excited.

We arrived at the hospital, and our ob/gyn was already in the maternity ward waiting for us. There was a frenetic, almost antsy energy crackling in the air as we checked in, but no different from what I previously had imagined all births and deliveries would somehow always elicit—pure adrenaline and serious hustle. Doctors and nurses shuffled past us briskly as we filled out all varieties of paperwork, while I tried to keep myself calm. As they wheeled Laura toward the delivery room, I like to believe, we were both feeling that we were about to take on adulthood in its most glorious form.

Things started to get complicated during the delivery, when the anesthesiologist began to have trouble getting the epidural placed properly. He tried a few times and just couldn't seem to get it right. The massive needle seemed to pierce Laura's lower back like a glass knife. She could see, through her watery eyes and lots of obvious physical pain, that I was starting to get nervous too. She became a bit edgy herself when she noticed that her back seemed to be completely drenched, realizing that the epidural fluid was leaking all over her.

Everything started to happen really fast at that point, a blurry series of abrupt clinical snapshots that I can barely decipher, but each one tinged with everyone's collective anxiety. Everything turned an even darker shade when the doctor announced that the baby's heart rate was slowing because the umbilical cord was wrapped around his little neck. I, now on the brink of fainting, pale as a ghost, and in a state of helpless shock, was clearly starting to lose it, to the point that Laura had to ask me to step out of the room and get a Coca-Cola. I couldn't stand to watch her suffer (and she couldn't stand to watch me watch her suffer), with that needle continuing to go in and out of her back, to no avail. The poor anesthesiologist was thrown out of the room as well, which is when the obstetrician said, "Forget about the epidural, this baby needs to come out *right now*." The baby was in distress, and so were we. By the time I was able to collect myself and come back into the room, they were already giving Laura an episiotomy, cutting her open from rectum to vagina with a local anesthetic, and with the help of forceps beginning to deliver our newborn son, Jorge Luis, who by now was totally bright purple. Poor Laura, who never once complained, was fully aware of everything that was happening, conscious of everyone in the room, and trying with all her might to control the situation from her position on the delivery bed. Her main concern, if you could imagine, was to take care of me.

After Jorge Luis was finally out, they abruptly took him off somewhere to run all the basic health tests. Since the doctor had had to cut Laura to help the delivery, he still had the task of stitching her up. But the major storm seemed to be over.

Later, when I saw Laura with the baby, a firstborn son who would carry my name, I felt utterly complete and perfectly whole. The adventure of a son–father relationship could mean so many things to me, and I really allowed myself to fantasize about how much fun it would all be. Everything seemed to be in sync, the scenes of my life playing out exactly as I had always dreamed they would. It was without a doubt one of the happiest days of my life.

CHAPTER 10

The Bittersweet Truth

Laura:

We waited about an hour or so, until finally a nurse came in holding the minuscule bundle of our son, who was warm, clean, and wrapped like a fresh little dumpling. My eyes fluttered open from the twilight nap that I'd gotten lost in, and there beside me was my husband, looking slightly nervous but smiling proudly, holding our first baby. We looked at him, both of us in tears, injected with the rawness of true, unconditional love. In the moments between shock, pain, deep sleep, and fuzzy wakefulness during my pregnancy, I had talked, dreamed, and fantasized about this first encounter with our son. Now, seeing him in Jorge's arms, I was beside myself with emotion. "What a vision," I thought blurrily through my fog of meds and exhaustion. Jorge passed the baby to me, and a wild blend of emotions overtook my being.

As hard as it is to admit—and I think I can only do so in hindsight—when I looked down at him on the day of his birth, despite the surge of love that I felt for him, I also instinctively knew that something was not quite right. The right front side of the baby's forehead looked slightly flat and even a bit caved in, and on the other side there was clearly a bump. I could not have imagined using these words then, but he looked visibly deformed. Jorge and I both saw and knew it right away. With just one look into each other's eyes, we said everything without speaking one word. We both knew there was something wrong, but neither of us wanted to be the one to say it first.

You have to remember that at this point we were both young, inexperienced, first-time parents, with no real point of reference as to "how things were supposed to be," so we just stayed sort of quiet under the unspoken assumption that the baby's head and face would gradually take proper shape. Of course we questioned the doctors and tried to get some clarity during those first few days, but everyone seemed to think we should just wait and see. There was no sense of desperation, no urgency, and no mad rush of physicians anxious about the way our child had been born.

The doctors simply told us that the use of forceps might have been the cause of the deformations but that we shouldn't worry—which of course is exactly what we wanted to hear. Needless to say, we were hungry for some semblance of relief after the crazy whirlwind of the delivery, and hearing the

doctors' casual response to what we thought might be a problem was almost music to our ears; indeed, we wanted to believe
that everything was under control, that forceps often cause slight
deformations, and that all we had to do was sit tight and all
would fall into place. But none of that happened, and two days
later we were discharged from the hospital, sent home with our
baby and a subtle but looming sense of dread. Looking back now,
it was a pure and total denial of the facts.

When we got home, I was still recovering from the debacle of the epidural, barely able to stand, dizzy from morning to
night, and aching from the whole ordeal. I was having chronic
postpartum headaches and felt nauseous most of the time. I tried
to breast-feed, but Jorge Luis could never seem to latch on properly, and each attempt left me (and probably him, as well) even
more frustrated and exhausted.

The worst part about it was that all throughout my own
debilitating physical misery, I could plainly see that Jorge Luis's
little head was still very much deformed. I would go to bed at
night, close my eyes, and silently pray that he would look normal the next morning when I'd go in to check on him. And
the following morning I would wake up, take a deep breath,
and drag myself over to his bassinette, only to see that nothing
had changed. I felt as if I were locked inside some awful dream,
the kind where you know you are dreaming and trying desperately to cry for help but no one seems to hear you no matter
how hard you scream. We didn't want to panic, but we knew we

would have to address the issue at some point. I guess we wanted to remain hopeful and not get all riled up, and we decided to believe that whatever it was, we would somehow be able to handle it. But by the tenth day, the baby still did not look quite right.

If my parents noticed anything unusual about his appearance, they did not say it to me and instead always displayed a silent optimism. They carried on as if everything were normal, and I suppose I was unconsciously waiting for someone to speak up and agree with me that something was not right. But no one had the heart to say it. *"Tapando el cielo con la mano,"* we say in Spanish. This metaphorically describes the act of trying to "cover the sky with your hand," which speaks to the notion of denial and the sense that reality is always right there, regardless of our conscious or unconscious attempts to hide it. But reality was getting closer and closer by the moment, and in time no amount of denial would be able to stifle what we were now up against.

The other thing was that the baby *never* stopped crying. He would cry from the moment he was awake to the moment he fell asleep, a screechy wail that pulsated through the whole house all day and all night. It was almost as if he himself knew that something was not right. We certainly did not know how to handle the crying and his evident discomfort and irritability, and that, combined with my painful recovery from the delivery, made those first few weeks seem impossible. There was no way of knowing if the baby was in pain or not, and if he was, we had no idea how to treat it. It definitely felt as though a crisis was brewing, but because of the newness of it all, neither of us knew exactly what we were dealing with. Each day seemed interminably long, the only constant being the perpetual shrieks of this poor child, who was clearly not well.

And then a few days later, we started to notice something else.

One day in December, I was holding the baby, during one of those very rare moments when he was quiet and calm, when I realized that not only was his head deformed, but it was also starting to look like one of his eyes was higher than the other one; worse still, his nose and mouth were both sort of off to the side as well. At first I thought that I was maybe hallucinating from lack of sleep, but the more I looked at him, the more I knew just how real it all was. I kept thinking that if it were indeed the use of forceps that had caused all of this, why was my baby's face shifting and morphing from one day to the next?

I used my own physical sickness as an excuse to keep friends and relatives, except for our parents, from visiting our house, frankly because I didn't want anyone to see him. I didn't want interrogations, I didn't want shame, and I definitely didn't want pity. Somehow I knew that a serious frenzy was coming, but I certainly did not want to be the one to start it.

CHAPTER 11

Facing the Music

Jorge:

I n Puerto Rico we have an expression, *"revolver la mierda,"* which literally means "stir the shit," which I guess is what we were afraid of doing by talking about things too much. Somehow it felt as if discussing it would only make things worse—or perhaps make it all that much more real—so for a moment we were left with our private, sad little mystery and all kinds of uncertainty. Our parents were among the very few people involved in any conversations about the baby, and though we kept generally quiet about our fears, we felt their concern, love, and support. They were practical in their assistance and helped us strategize and focus, despite the emotions that clearly came with all our doubt. They knew we were afraid, but they also knew not to make it worse by panicking themselves. They needed to show us strength so that we could move forward to understand exactly what was happening.

Laura's father had a cousin who was a well-known local pediatrician, so we thought it would be a good idea to take Jorge Luis to him for an examination. My father-in-law accompanied us to the doctor and, after the consultation, patiently waited with the baby in the reception area while the doctor spoke with us. Laura's cousin took one look at our son and said, "I don't want to scare you guys, but I think I saw this before when I did a rotation at New York University. I think I know just the specialist you should see." Though he was trying to keep cool, there definitely seemed to be a sense of urgency to his tone, and the specificity of his diagnostic suspicions alarmed and relieved me at the same time. On the one hand, if we knew what it was, we could figure out how to fix it; but on the other hand, what if it was something that simply could not be fixed?

The doctor immediately took X-rays of the baby's head, and the glaring deformities were evident to everyone who saw the films. "Let me make a few calls," he said. "I really suggest you go see Dr. Joseph McCarthy right away." The doctor was adamant in a way that made us know instantly that we had better heed his advice. Of course he sensed our trepidation and didn't want to say anything concrete just yet. Instead, he insisted that Dr. McCarthy was the absolutely best person to consult with on the matter and that we would be best served by being directly under his care and authority. He assured us that we would be in excellent hands and that if this were in fact what he suspected it was, Dr. McCarthy would be the one who could tell us exactly what to do. We left the pediatrician's office half hopeful and half crushed. I did not know whether to stay optimistic that we were at least on some kind of path or to dread what we might find at the end of it. Even though we had seen a doctor, there now seemed to be more questions than answers. What could this mysterious condition be? What could be so specific that it required us to take our newborn on an emergency trip to Manhattan? Why could the pediatrician not lay it out for us? Were we dealing with something rare? Was this somehow all going to go away miraculously? There was no way to even begin addressing all of our concerns. And though our baby was just over a week old, Laura and I decided to fly to New York immediately.

Manuel Mendez (Laura's father):

*T*he way I was raised, for me to really get scared, the sky would have to actually be falling right out of the sky. We were raised to face things, to look at problems eye to eye, without wallowing in fear, to use our energy to strategize and overcome, and to always try to live within this system of fortitude—a system that I very consciously taught my own children. Now I somehow knew that my daughter would need all of our strength, and I chose, right there and then, to tap into my own reservoir of power so that I could be one of the rocks that she and her husband could lean on as we continued to try to figure this thing out.

I don't like to use the word "denial," but that may have been the world we were living in during those first few weeks. No one wants to believe that his child could be sick, and the adult mind is capable of all kinds of trickery when faced with serious fear and helplessness. The truth is that we did not know how to react. Our instinct was to stay quietly resilient and try as best as possible to believe that things would ultimately fall into place. We were holding on to the fact that Dr. Joseph McCarthy was the preeminent authority on cases like our son's, so we felt that at least we would be in the right hands and that we were on the right path.

And on what seemed like one of the most chilling winter nights of our lives, we flew back to New York City with our ten-day-old baby, this little peanut of a human, totally defenseless. We bundled and swaddled Jorge Luis in all kinds of layers and blankets and made sure to keep him close to our chests, wrapped tightly in our arms. No matter what was happening, the most important thing for both of us from the beginning of the whole ordeal was that he always feel protected and secure. The flight seemed eternal, with the air pressure in the cabin weighing down on what already felt like a pretty heavy situation. We couldn't eat or drink a thing, and though we tried to close our eyes to rest for a bit, neither of us could even remotely sink into relaxation mode. Our nerves had utterly taken over the situation, and nothing but the knowledge that our baby would be okay could give us any comfort. We held hands, but we didn't talk much—again, feeling that discussing things too much would somehow make them even more intense. We just went through the motions, doing what we had to do, and hoping for the best—a system that we would come to rely on for many years that followed.

The next morning, we sat with our son in the waiting room of the Langone Medical Center at NYU. There was an uncomfortable heaviness in the room that neither of us had ever experienced, a feeling of impending doom that we could not begin to understand or even articulate to each other. The fact was that we had flown all the way from Puerto Rico to New York on the encouragement of Laura's cousin, who was an experienced and well-regarded doctor. Though he had hesitated to give a definite diagnosis, he had certainly not shown any hesitation in sending us to New York. Like us, he knew that something grave was happening to our baby. Whatever it was that we were facing, given the circumstances, it had to be serious. Laura held Jorge Luis as if it were the last time she would get the chance. The "not-knowing factor" was so strong that our imaginations ran wild with all kinds of terrifying possibilities. I could see that she was fighting back tears, that she didn't want our son, despite his being a baby, to see that his mama was hurting and scared. No matter how bad things ever got, Laura would always show him strength, which of course inspired and impressed me—but never surprised me.

Dr. McCarthy himself came out to the reception area to greet us and escort us in. His eyes went directly to the baby, his mind obviously processing everything right there before us. With a subtle nod of his head and a slight grimace of his lips, it was clear to us that he already knew what he was looking at. Mortified in advance of whatever was going to come out of his mouth, we just looked at each other in silence.

"Yep, that's craniosynostosis," the doctor proclaimed, saying the word as if we already knew what it meant. He could tell that we were as clueless as we were afraid and asked us to join him in his office, where we could talk the whole thing through. Dr. McCarthy proceeded to describe our son's disease to us in what seemed like a language from another planet. He said that our son was suffering from a skull deformity caused by the premature closure of the fibrous joints in his head—which essentially meant that his brain was growing and developing without adequate space in his skull.

We asked the doctor to explain the scenario as simply as possible, but no matter how clearly he did so, we could not rationally or emotionally digest the information he was delivering. The idea that our son could be suffering from a disease of the skull was not something either of us could have imagined, and now that we knew, the ramifications of such an illness seemed even more harrowing than the not knowing.

Millions of questions were racing in our minds: Did a skull disease mean our baby could have brain damage? Did this mean he would not be able to lead a normal life? Had they given us the wrong baby in Puerto Rico? Was all of this a bad dream?

Why was this happening to us? Were we being punished for something? Did we not handle the pregnancy properly? Was our son's life ruined? Was our chance at parenting completely shot? Would we be able to take care of him properly? Would he require special attention? Would our son's world from now on always be made up of doctors and hospitals? Was he in pain? Was he suffering? Would he always suffer? Did that mean we were destined to suffer eternally too? Would our lives, as we knew them, essentially be over? After everything that we had been through already, it was so hard to imagine that this was only going to be the beginning. It felt like a category 5 hurricane of questions, shock, and guilt—and we did not have even one umbrella between the two of us.

CHAPTER 12

The Darkness

Hiding in my room, safe within my womb,
I touch no one and no one touches me.
—PAUL SIMON

Laura:

Because we knew nothing about the disease at this point, we could not possibly understand the extent of its reach (never mind how involved our family would ultimately become with it). We were already so worn out: imagine traveling to New York in the freezing cold with a sick, ten-day-old baby and arriving to discover that in reality you can't even *begin* to help this poor little creature that you've been doing your best to bundle up and keep warm. It was a feeling of total helplessness, desperation, and defeat, something neither of us had ever really felt before. Though I had only been a mother now for a little over a week,

I was starting to have a sinking feeling that I would not be able to help my child. I had never failed at anything before, and I was terrified about the possibility of failing as a parent.

After a thorough examination of Jorge Luis, Dr. McCarthy confirmed the diagnosis of craniosynostosis, even saying that this case appeared to be severe.

"Severe?" I thought. Things were already bad enough; how could our baby's condition be any more severe than we imagined? How could things possibly get worse? He said that we could do nothing until the baby was at least nine months old, when it would be possible to perform the necessary, albeit elaborate, twelve-hour craniofacial surgery to essentially reconstruct his head. He calmly explained to us that the surgeon would open the baby's skull from ear to ear, peel back the skin, cut out and reshape the bones, place them back in, and resew his head. All of this on the head of our nine-month-old infant was just not something that we could fathom. And not only was there the idea of the gruesome operation to contend with but nine entire months to sit and stew in the anxiety of it all, helpless and devoid of any better alternatives.

As the doctor spoke to us, I remember looking at my husband's eyes. I knew his eyes would tell me if I really needed to worry. He sat steady, listening to Dr. McCarthy's straightforward explanation, taking all of it in as a noisy clock ticked behind us in what seemed like the coldest room in the world. I was there too, but my mind was not; all of my thoughts were off somewhere, desperately trying to figure out what I had done to deserve this and digesting the flurry of questions that bombarded my mind. All I could process was that clock ticking, that chill air, and my own heartbeat, now heavy in my chest. I was totally broken.

Hearing that horrendous seven-syllable word for the first time was probably the toughest thing. You hear it—*craniosyn-ostosis*—and you wonder, what in God's name can that possibly mean? Cranium equals brain, so of course you think the worst. The doctor also told us that because of the way the head continues to grow and develop as the child does, this is the kind of disease that might require regular maintenance—"touch-ups," as the routine surgical procedures are referred to—and that the initial surgery could very well be his first of many.

We weren't sure whether to believe the doctor or not, whether we should scour the medical community for second, third, and fourth opinions—or if we should accept the news and move on to figure out how we were going to deal with it. With a new baby in your arms, you want to be hopeful, not live in a constant state of dread. For a long time, I blocked the entire conversation out of my mind—maybe it was my unconscious way of not wanting to remember how horrible it made me feel. My entire world was now unraveling right under my nose, and my tiny, defenseless little boy was getting the brunt of it. I felt so incredibly robbed of the chance to experience that baby-love gush that first-time parents get to have—the sunny sweet bliss fest that comes when a child is born. Our lives were laced with panic and shock, which for a while would color the entire atmosphere in our home.

We could not help wondering if it had been our fault somehow, so we ended up taking all kinds of genetic tests to see if Jorge Luis might somehow have inherited the condition from one of us; but the results were negative, and it became clear that his case was of the nongenetic variety, the kind that occurs haphazardly with no rhyme or reason, "a glitch of nature," as it was explained to us.

Jorge and I quickly learned that one of the most baffling things about the illness is the challenge of trying to ascertain its trigger or to even know how long or elaborate the treatment will be; weeks, years, months, there is just no way to know—and this type of infinite waiting and wondering has the power to drive any parent into a world of immeasurable anxiety. Knowing that we were dealing with a cranial disorder, all I could think about was how the baby's brain would be affected, his motor skills, if he would ever be able to walk, run, and do the things that we had always done and loved to do as kids ourselves.

Our doctors rightfully did not want to scare us, so they tried not to focus on the worst-case scenarios. But we now know that the potentially dangerous developments included a wide range of horrendous outcomes (the most awful of those possibilities being brain damage, which we feared intensely). Instead, our doctors urged us to remain positive, explaining that the diagnosis and treatment of craniosynostosis is extremely time-sensitive and that the earlier the diagnosis is made, the sooner a plan for treatment can be put into action. They helped us understand the importance of the initial surgery that loomed gloomily in our future and made us see that the procedure would set the entire scope of our son's treatment into motion.

We went back to Puerto Rico determined to make the best of it, to stay positive; however, the months leading up to the operation were incredibly difficult. My husband and I continued to not discuss our dilemma at length and focused only on loving our son, on playing with him and spending as much time with him as we could. We spoke about the logistics, but we certainly did not dwell on them. It was definitely an odd state of affairs: we didn't talk about it at dinner, and we didn't talk about it in bed. The proverbial elephant was undoubtedly in the room, but I suppose our silence was our way of standing strong and keeping our life as normal as we could.

But things were very rough. Jorge Luis didn't stop crying, and we had no clue what we were doing as parents. We didn't even know how to change a diaper or how to feed him. Because of how crazy things had gotten immediately after the birth, I for some reason abandoned my initial plan to hire some help. Perhaps this was because I felt the need to somehow take control of the situation in the way that I had always known how to do—by myself. I also didn't want help now because I didn't want anyone to see him, to know that there was something wrong with him. I didn't want to answer the phone or face my friends, who of course were all eager to know what was going on.

Up to that point in our lives, I had considered myself the type of person who could handle anything. I had always been able to get things done, to figure them out. But now I found myself clueless and daunted. I was so afraid of failing as a parent, but the circumstances, as they were then, became so much bigger than me.

I would spend entire days in my pajamas, with no time to cook, shower, or to take care of my own things. Before all of this, I had become delightfully accustomed to doing everything for my husband, as he was my *consentido,* as we say in Spanish, meaning the one I would always love to pamper and spoil. I used to leave him sweet little notes scribbled on toilet paper; I would write out menus of special foods that I knew he would adore and serve them to him during candlelit dinners—but as things were now, I didn't even have two seconds to make the man a sandwich.

Liliana (Laura's close friend):

I never wanted to ask what was going on, because it was very clear from the get-go that something was wrong with the baby, but Jorge and Laura were very private, and of course, as her friends, we all wanted to respect that. We girls would talk among ourselves, asking if anyone had talked to Laura or knew what was happening, because we could all pick up on the fact that something heavy was going on. But we didn't want to bother them and gave them their space, hoping that in time we would find out what was happening and be able to show support however we could.

Jorge, at the time, was playing the winter league in Puerto Rico, so I didn't have a car. I was home alone all day long. One of our mothers would come to visit now and again, and that was my only contact with the outside world. I stayed locked in the house, shrouded in darkness, trying to make my baby stop crying. Every day seemed exactly like the last, where nothing changed except for how bad I felt. I was in some kind of mourning, feeling that the light of the sun would blind me if I dared to go out. It was a bleak desperation unlike anything I had ever known before. I didn't even recognize myself. Gone was the girl who had longed to work, play, laugh, dance, and socialize—and in her place now stood a stunted, petrified new mother with no direction, no answers, and very little hope.

CHAPTER 13

Hiding in Secrecy

We dance round in a ring and suppose,
but the secret sits in the middle and knows.
—ROBERT FROST

Jorge:

N ow that we knew that we were not genetic carriers
and that our son had, in fact, randomly presented with
craniosynostosis, we were desperate to figure out how or why
this could have happened. When I was not playing or training,
I would scour the Internet, search encyclopedias, read books—
whatever I could do to learn about the disease. Remember that
I was in (pre-Google) Puerto Rico, where cases like this were
extremely rare. Craniosynostosis just wasn't an illness people
really knew about, so there did not seem to be a whole lot of
information on it. I learned a bit online, but even then I didn't

feel that I really understood the disease. I didn't have a sense of when (or even *if*) there was going to be a light at the end of the tunnel. Through our hospital we were put into contact with other families who were dealing with the illness, but neither Laura nor I felt comfortable with the idea of sharing this new family secret with total strangers. We decided to hold our son's baptism in February 2000, in the privacy of only our own closest family members, an intimate ceremony where we would, in our own quiet way, express our love and prayers.

I didn't want the media attention, and I did not want my son's illness to become an excuse in regard to the quality of my playing. But most important, we didn't want people to make fun of him or feel sorry for us. So in those early weeks and months we kept him inside a lot and tried to keep the whole ordeal as quiet and private as possible.

I did, however, confide in my good friend Benjamin in Puerto Rico, and, of course, I also told a few of my teammates. Gerald Williams, Derek Jeter, Tino Martinez, and Joe Torre all knew what was happening, and like brothers they stuck by me, helped keep it quiet, and gave me the support I needed so that I could be strong for my family. I would talk to them during practices or in the locker room, simply telling them what was unfolding at home and even admitting to them how scary it really was. Though none of them could give me an answer, just venting to them about the situation gave me some degree of relief. They always asked for updates and wanted to stay closely

Tino Martinez (fellow New York Yankee):

*H*e would tell us what was going on, because the media didn't know . . . he was open and explained everything, and the prognosis always seemed to be good. He made it sound like everything was going to be fine. You could tell he was worried, but at least he tried to stay positive when he talked about it to us.

posted on the status of my son. Men show emotion in radically different ways from women, and sometimes just having those close few buddies around was enough to get me through the day.

Thirty days passed and the baby still looked horribly deformed, so more and more we began to resign ourselves to the reality of what was happening. We still didn't know much about the disease, but we knew that sometime in the next nine months, our son's head would be opened from ear to ear. There was no real planning we could do, no scheme we could magically set into motion. Though we had always prided ourselves on success through strategy, there was not enough strategizing in the world to help plan for what was coming. All we could do was wait and pray that the surgery that awaited our baby would somehow make all of this go away. The only thing we *did* know with certainty was that we were at the mercy of something awful.

At a time like this, what should have been a silver lining— our real wedding in Puerto Rico—was also now becoming an obstacle. Remember that before Jorge Luis was born we were deep in the throes of planning our proper wedding for three hundred guests made up of close friends and family for a party that by now neither of us really wanted to have. The notion of celebrating seemed so contrary to everything we were experiencing. Because we still had not really publicized our son's condition, it seemed like an impossible feat to get through the wedding without having to address it. How could we possibly be happy at our wedding with this at the forefront of our lives? We felt guilty about experiencing any sense of joy under the circumstances of Jorge Luis's illness, never mind organizing and coordinating the logistics. We simply didn't know how we were going to get through it.

About a week before the wedding we were invited to Laura's parents' house for dinner. As we sat around the table to start the meal, out of nowhere Laura just broke down and cried. "I can't do this," she wept. "I need help, I'm hurting, and I'm sick. I don't know how to take care of my son, I am so powerless." She continued to sob, the words spilling out of her like toxins, seeming to free up some space in her devastated soul. I don't think I had ever seen her express such vulnerability before; but honestly, we all knew that she had pretty much been awake for two months steady by now, and that the baby's crying, the stamp of his diagnosis, and the impending surgery were all gradually chipping away at the last shreds of her peace of mind. My in-laws and I just sat there staring at Laura, and she knew that we all felt exactly the way she did. It was a collective helplessness. It's as if we were all saying, "How could we all just keep faking it?"

Laura's mother put her arms around her and said, "Don't worry, we're going to get you all the help you need; whatever is going to happen is going to happen, but first you need to take care of yourself." She called a woman named Carmen who had taken care of Laura's grandmother, a Spanish woman who could help us with the baby during the night. Here was Laura's dame of a mother, once again, to hold her hand and support her when she needed it the most. With our parents' old-world sensibilities, they were always the first ones to step up when anything in our lives needed attention. Hearing the confidence in Laura's mother's tone calmed me down, and I could see that the panic that had frozen my wife into immobility was now, thanks to her mom, also starting to thaw. Maybe it was the flash of love and gratitude for her mother that flipped an inner switch, telling her that she too would always instinctively want to support our own children this way. And to properly do that, Laura's mother was right: we would need to take care of ourselves first.

With Carmen's help during the nights, Laura finally started to get a bit of sleep. She also started working out again, which became the driving force of her battle against depression. We would exercise together, a quiet but collective blowing off of steam, moving, breathing, and energizing that would somehow get us through the day. Having been a fitness model, she had felt it important to get her figure back soon after the birth, but because of the way things had gone, fitness had seemed like a shallow indulgence. But she quickly realized that exercise was the healthiest thing she could do, and it is exactly what started to pull her out of the black hole that she had been living inside. She learned how imperative it was to carve out some time for herself, be it for exercise, yoga, meditation, dancing—anything that could give her a healthy escape. We both started to understand that if you don't feel good, you are prone to give off a weak energy to your kids, which is something we never wanted to do. Her exercise time became a one-stop experience where she could get fit, healthy, and sane. It got her out of the house, and the endorphins she released somehow helped quell her chronic sorrow and gradually ease her back to strength (which, God knows, we would need).

ABOVE: *Jorge, age 4, with his mother, Tamara Posada, in Puerto Rico*

BELOW LEFT: *Jorge, age 6, in his elementary school uniform*

BELOW RIGHT: *Little Laura, age 3, smiles for the camera*

ABOVE LEFT:
Laura, age 14, with her arsenal of trophies

ABOVE RIGHT:
Jorge, age 23, in his early days on the baseball diamond

LEFT:
Laura and Jorge on an early date in New York

*Laura and Jorge's
wedding in Puerto Rico*

*Laura, pregnant with Jorge
Luis, and Jorge in the New
York ticker-tape parade*

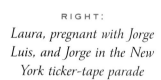

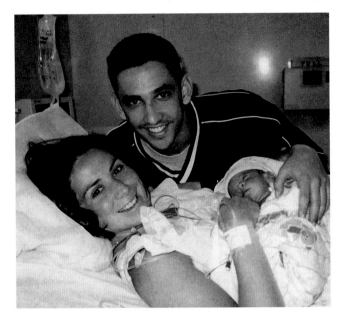

ABOVE: *Jorge Luis is born in Puerto Rico in 1999*

BELOW: *Jorge Luis's first birthday in Puerto Rico*

Laura and Jorge Luis in Tampa, Florida

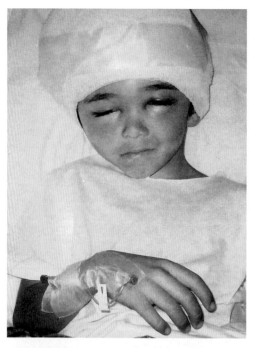

LEFT:
Jorge Luis after
his last surgery

BELOW:
Jorge Luis and Laura
share a moment after
the last surgery

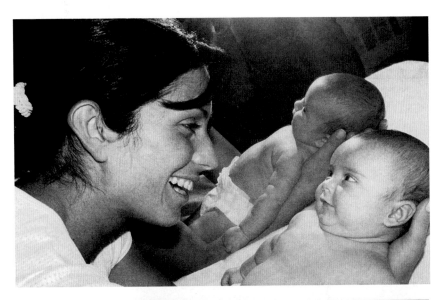

ABOVE:
*Laura shares a
laugh with baby
Paulina*

RIGHT:
*Jorge after a swim
with Jorge Luis
and Paulina*

The Posada family on vacation in 2009

PART IV

Burdens and Blessings

Suffering is but another name for teaching of experience,
which is the parent of instruction and the schoolmaster of life.

—HORACE (ANCIENT ROMAN POET)

CHAPTER 14

In Sickness and in Health

Laura:

With my new exercise regimen in place, I felt a bit more relaxed and was able to make another important mental switch: I decided that our wedding should not be something to dread and that instead we should look at it as a wonderful opportunity to celebrate our union with our closest friends and family. Didn't we need just that? Didn't we need all the love we could get? We made up our minds that although it felt horribly awkward to celebrate during a time like this, maybe it was God's way of hinting to us that we should make the most out of the situation, and if our wedding was going to be a shimmer of light in this dark and strange abyss, maybe that wouldn't be so bad. We shifted the agony of the whole thing to acceptance and even appreciation of the things in our lives that *were* worthy of celebration.

The day of my wedding, I made the decision to have a good time no matter what. I thought, "I owe it to myself, my son, and my husband to stay positive and be happy, if only for this one day." I swigged a few cocktails before the ceremony, so by the time my hair was getting blow-dried and styled I was already toasting with myself. Unlike at the wedding ceremony in New York, when I could barely make it out of the bathroom without fainting at the thought of holy matrimony, this time around I had somehow softened. Life's new circumstances, awful as they seemed, were perhaps beginning to chisel away at my selfishness. Now I could not imagine handling anything without my husband and never questioned the fact that he was my destined partner, for better or for worse. It's amazing how quickly things can change, but I knew that on this special January day our wedding would mean so much more than just the celebration of two people in love. This wedding symbolized the notion that Jorge and I would be steadfast companions moving forward together, to be there for each other for every step of the way. When I arrived at the altar, Jorge whispered, "I've never seen you look so beautiful" and looked at me exactly the way you want a man to look at you when you are about to marry him. For that split second, we were again on top of the world.

We really wanted our son to be there, but as sad as it was for us to admit, we didn't want anyone to see him. So we had Carmen stay with him and then arrive at the church later, after all the guests had already been seated. She held him close, keeping him

Liliana (Laura's friend):

I had arrived a bit late for the ceremony, and though I knew that Laura was trying to keep the baby hidden, I sneaked my way around the church and found a way to take a peek at him. From my perspective, it was clear there was something wrong with the baby when I saw him that day. But Laura was my friend, and the last thing I was going to do was ruin her wedding day by saying something about it. Also, although it clearly looked as if the baby was somehow deformed, I knew that babies are often born with little physical quirks that correct themselves, so I wanted to stay positive and assume that was going to be the case for Laura and Jorge's son.

quiet and calm in a separate room in the church, while we, his parents, were exchanging vows in the other room. I know that some of our closest friends did in fact try to get a peek at him somehow, if only to finally meet the little guy, which everyone (not knowing what was going on) was eager to do. But if anyone did in fact see him, they were respectful and gracious enough to keep their comments to themselves, something I appreciated tremendously. As it was, despite the joy of my wedding, I was having a really hard time knowing that my baby was sick.

It was such a delicate secret we were harboring, but we knew that our silence was our way of protecting him. We knew that if we told anyone, the media would not leave us alone. Our life would turn into a circus, although for all intents and purposes, it already was. We knew that any admission of our son's disease would make things considerably more stressful. We also knew that because of the nature of the disease and the way Jorge Luis looked, if photos of him started circulating, people would not stop talking. And we certainly did not want anyone thinking (never mind saying) that our son was a freak. We just didn't want to be front-page news.

At the altar, my husband and I knew that he was there with us, and I guess that was all that really mattered. As the ceremony ended, the baby was sneaked out as quietly and quickly as he had been sneaked in, and I managed to dodge every question about him. Jorge and I made our way out of the church, while our guests held a massive canopy of baseball bats in formation over our heads. It was truly fantastic, and, all obvious logistical and emotional challenges aside, our wedding day was actually beautiful.

After the wedding, we reluctantly went to the Bahamas for four days. We left the baby with our parents and Carmen, but the whole time, we just wanted to get back home. We felt guilty, resisting the urge to enjoy what was meant to be our honeymoon. My husband and I had a strong sense that we needed to be with Jorge Luis every moment of his (potentially short) life. We did not know if he would make it past the surgery in seven months, so in our minds, every moment that we didn't spend with him was another special moment that we might miss.

Derek Jeter (fellow New York Yankee):

I too was one of the ones who managed to see little Jorge at their wedding. I knew they were trying to keep him under wraps, but being so close to Jorge, I was eager to finally meet his son. I was able to figure out that their nanny was watching the baby and made it a point to find out where she was. I understood that Jorge and Laura wanted their privacy, because it was clear they didn't really want people seeing Jorge Luis, but because of my friendship with Jorge, I already felt close to the boy. As much as I hate to say it, as soon as I did see the baby, I knew right away that there was something wrong. Needless to say, I was concerned. It was their wedding day, so obviously I didn't want to bring it up or sit around and talk about something scary or intense on what was supposed to be the happiest day of their lives. I had known Jorge long enough to know that he would open up to me more when the time was right.

Maybe I didn't really understand what love was until this baby was born, because I never wanted to be apart from him. I felt that my attention to and presence for him were the only true comfort that I could provide him. He would fall asleep in my lap, his favorite place to relax, and the moment I put him in the crib he would start to whimper and cry. I didn't know if he was

Tia Doris (Laura's aunt):

*L*aura was incredibly anxious a lot of the time and definitely afraid. I remember her telling me that this was the hardest thing she'd ever experienced, looking straight at me with the saddest eyes in the world. I would plead with her to come to church, but she was never the religious type, so she'd say no. Still, I tried to show my support for her however I could. One thing is certain: Laura never wanted to separate from her son. She was determined to make sure he was okay at all hours of the day and night, at the risk of her own very steady insomnia. I always knew Laura to be totally self-sufficient, and I also knew very well that she would not easily relinquish control over any situation, especially not where her family was concerned.

But there were so many sleepless nights where the baby would cry all night, and eventually Laura would call me for help. I would arrive at her house and find her in a state of frantic desperation, totally broken down and incredibly anxious for some relief. It was clear that she needed help, and I was glad to be able to be the one to give it.

in pain or what it was that was making him suffer so much. But I knew exactly in which position to recline so that he could be the most relaxed and comfortable. We connected intensely this way. I cannot tell you how many photos we have of Jorge Luis asleep on my lap with his little legs crossed like a small rotisserie chicken.

The only other thing that always calmed him down was music. He could be in the most awful mood, fussy and irritable no end, but if I played some classical music he would instantly relax. The moment he would hear the sounds, his little body would soften, his eyes would close, and his breathing would steady. It was like clockwork. It moved me so much that even a child with his kind of problem could appreciate the power and impact of a soulful sound. It somehow assured me that my son was all right and that, hard as things were, I still had the capacity to acknowledge the precious moments when they arose.

When we returned home from the bittersweet honeymoon, happy as we were to be reunited with our son, we slipped right back into our old loop of despair, waiting nervously for the next seven months before anything could really change.

I began to get increasingly irritable and cranky, with a sinking feeling that nothing would ever feel right. It got so bad that Jorge had to leave me alone a lot. He would say, "I can't deal with this. I have to go," which would of course infuriate me, because how could he leave at a time like that? But in hindsight I know that he was really discombobulated too, and neither of us knew how else to deal. His career needed attention, which I also understood. But he was scared, just like me. When you have a newborn baby, it is supposed to be the happiest time of your life. For us it was the complete opposite. Instead of a joy, at times it felt like a punishment. Despite the momentary bliss of our wedding and honeymoon, there was a quiet, unspoken tension in our home that stayed every night and remained there each morning. We simply did not know what to do with our love for our baby. There it was: our love—shining, enormous, and glowing—for our firstborn son, and we had absolutely no idea what to do with it. The possibility of losing him was always in the room, and there was never anything anyone could say or do to make that better.

The next few months went by like single drops of water, one by one, leaking slowly from a faucet that wasn't turned off all the way. I spent every possible waking minute with Jorge Luis, save for the time I allowed myself a workout, which was the only thing that kept me sane. But the phone was starting to ring off the hook; my friends now wanted answers, and more than anything, they wanted to make sure I was okay.

I remember the day my good friend Liliana called me to tell me the awful news that her own sister had been killed in a car accident. For some reason, hearing Liliana's grief, seeing her so exposed, I felt the need to tell her about Jorge Luis and his craniosynostosis, for the first time opening up about it to someone outside of my immediate family. I told her how I too felt that

Liliana (Laura's friend):

When Laura and I spoke after my sister's death, she not only relayed her heartfelt condolences, but she also, for the first time, completely broke down into a fit of sobbing and tears and vented to me about her own tribulations with the baby. I'd had a serious hunch that something was amiss, especially after I had sneakily seen him at their wedding, but hearing Laura open up about it now made me realize just how serious things really were.

She finally shared with me the news about his health problems and everything that she and her husband were enduring. Laura had never been the type of woman to break down and cry—she was always strong and totally held together—but it was clear that she had now reached her emotional threshold. She hysterically told me that she felt like she was going crazy, that Jorge Luis would never stop crying, that she hadn't been sleeping, that she didn't know how this could be happening or how they were going to get through any of it. While she spoke, I could even hear Jorge Luis wailing in the background, and I could tell that her world was really coming apart at the seams. She sounded as disheveled as I felt, as I was dealing with my own grief then, but I know it was probably good for her to finally release some of the burden that she was carrying around in total isolation.

my son had somehow died and that in a way I felt like a walking corpse myself, devoid of any joy or peace, a zombie of sadness. It was scary, but it was also a tremendous relief to talk about it. She was in total shock, as my reaction to her loss came out as pure empathy and commiseration, the two of us bound in a mutual vulnerability.

CHAPTER 15

Keeping Your Eye on the Ball

Jorge:

I decided to go to Tampa even though it was a bit early for spring training, which, as you can imagine, enraged Laura. Since we had been together, we had made a very conscious effort never to separate, so leaving her alone with Jorge Luis at a time like that was pretty agonizing. However, the stress was killing us, and I thought (though Laura didn't necessarily agree) that maybe a bit of distance might alleviate the heaviness. The honest truth is that I did not know how to handle the situation, so the vibe between us as a couple was starting to feel tense. When we talked on the phone, I could hear her desperation, and I would do my best to assure her that things were going to somehow work out, but of course how could I really know that? She was rightfully livid at the fact that I had abandoned her and the baby at such a time and at first even refused to come to Tampa. I guess I was trying to hold on to the fact that they were going to operate on him in August and was just looking forward to moving on.

Thankfully, Laura did eventually change her mind and decided to fly to Tampa with the baby. Though the air weighed heavy on us and the tensions felt high, she came because she knew we would have to stick together as a family to make it through the next few months until the surgery. It was one of those moments when we both knew that we would have to wrangle our emotions for the sake of our family. Those were the times I knew we had what it would take as a couple to survive the ordeal—equal parts faith in each other, endless passion, and total respect. Our relationship always made me feel that we were truly each other's best friends and gave me the security to plow forward as a father, a husband, and a ballplayer. Through the hardest moments and even when I was really far away, I knew that Laura always felt my love.

———————

After the spring training in Tampa, we went to New York for the season, and things got even more intense. Now we were closer to the surgery, so there were logistics to deal with, and our world quickly became one of doctors, charts, tests, records, and hospitals. For starters, we were told that Jorge Luis would require three blood transfusions for the surgery, which at first seemed to pose a challenge, given the baby's blood type, O negative, the rarest kind. We were terrified of having to get the blood from a bank, envisioning the horrendous possibilities involving transmissible diseases. Thankfully, because of my blood type, O negative, it was decided that I would be a suitable donor, but it was hard to keep my cool, when everything seemed like such a tremendous risk. This little creature was not even a year old, and he was being run through machines, his blood taken, and his innocent eyes already exposed to the brutal reality of disease and pain. It was a really difficult thing to watch, and I had to constantly remind myself to hold it together.

And at the risk of sounding shallow in the face of such serious family matters, I have to admit that baseball was essential for me. Not only was it my way of blowing off steam, but you also have to remember that it was also very much my job. This is my livelihood, and in the baseball industry, you're expected to be on the field and in training, by any means necessary. The bosses expect you to perform, and they expect you to be good. I felt that I should keep working and tried to hold on to the belief that perhaps my commitment to playing could make me stronger for my family. In playing, I thought, I could remain steady, providing a sturdy foundation on which to anchor the life together we were facing.

Just being on the field made me feel supported, and once I was in a game, I could try to slip into the zone and just be part of the team machine, and maybe even disappear for a moment into the reality of the play. But even when I gave everything to my game, I was always thinking about Jorge Luis and Laura.

Catching is a position that requires a lot of concentration, and a lot of times, my brain was a total jumble. I remember striking out twice in a game and not giving a damn. I would get to the stadium and stay totally quiet. I just wasn't there. I remember once playing a game in Toronto and I was so irritable, I argued with the umpire and basically got thrown out of the game. That was the first time anything like that had ever happened to me, so it was definitely a low point. In general, although I used baseball as a kind of escape, I don't remember hitting, I don't remember catching, and I don't even remember being at many of those games. What I do remember from that time are scenes from all of

Derek Jeter (fellow New York Yankee):

*T*hough he didn't talk about it a lot, Jorge is certainly not the kind of guy who is going to make excuses for playing a less-than-perfect game. But it had to have affected his mind on the field. How could it not? I think playing ball was a way for him to release. Laura, being the mom, was with the baby every single moment. She never left the kid's sight. So Jorge had to be strong for her. He stayed quiet, but he played the game hard and stayed focused.

Tino Martinez (fellow New York Yankee):

Y ou have to remember that playing with the New York Yankees comes with a lot of pressure. It's the greatest team in the world to play for, but it does not come without a price. For every single game that you play, you're essentially under a microscope. Every time you don't play well, there are at least fifty or sixty writers out there who are just waiting to tear you apart in the papers, and you have to be able to deal with all the negative press written about you. Usually, when a player makes a mistake, it's no big deal, but when you're playing for the Yankees, everyone is watching. So I would imagine that Jorge was carrying a heavy burden, especially around the time of the surgery.

the different medical procedures that Jorge Luis had to endure, seeing my little son all rigged up, hooked up to a million tubes, getting MRIs, CAT scans, and blood tests, and time moving so incredibly slowly. I was so distracted by my family crisis that season, I honestly don't know how the Yankees won the World Series that year, let alone how I myself was able to perform.

Finally, after what seemed like an interminable amount of time, July came and our son was finally ready to undergo the procedure that would allegedly save him. We had had plenty of time to prepare mentally, and we decided to face the surgery with every last ounce of strength we could muster. We knew what we had to do, and we were now as ready as we would ever be to face it head-on. It was a quiet faith that we shared, and though we didn't talk, I know we both felt it. We wanted our son to see us strong, present, and available—and we wanted him to always feel that his roots were solid and firm. But it was certainly not easy.

CHAPTER 16

Unimaginable Solutions

Laura:

The days and nights were starting to feel eternal. I had totally lost contact with the world and could barely grasp the quickly unfolding reality of our situation. During those nine months, as I waited for a horrendous-sounding procedure to change the outcome of my family's life, I waged my internal emotional battle in total solitude. I rarely expressed to my husband how I honestly felt, and usually I would spend the day with a rehearsed smile pretending that everything was fine. I was furious with him for leaving me alone so abruptly when he left for Tampa even before spring training began but ultimately forgave him because I understood that, like me, he was having a difficult time digesting our son's delicate situation. For the most part, I didn't really share my feelings with other relatives or friends either, since I felt I was somehow alone with the disease and no one else could possibly understand how I felt. Things went on like that, as I ignored the aforementioned elephant that was always in the room—until the day before the surgery, when I sobbed hysterically in the shower, praying for my son's life, praying that this would not be the last night I would get to tuck him in to go to sleep. I was holding on to the fact that maybe after this surgery, Jorge Luis would begin to finally recover and that perhaps he would at last stop crying. I honestly believed that he was in some kind of pain that he could not articulate, which was an awful thing to come to terms with. Perhaps the surgery would address whatever it was that was making him suffer, and that alone allowed me to follow through with our plan the next morning.

However, no part of this delicate moment came without serious soul-searching. The next day, as we drove to the hospital toward the unimaginable, that dreaded flurry of unanswerable questions came back to haunt me. Was it my fault? What could I have done to avoid this? Was I being punished for something? Was there a chance that he would really die? Had I already failed as a mother? Those and so many more inquiries resurfaced as I held my son close to my chest—my effort to transmit as much love as I could to him before what I imagined might likely be the end of his life. I didn't know how else to handle the situation other than to hug him with all of my soul poured into my embrace and to keep him physically and metaphorically as close to my own heart as possible.

After the hustle of checking in and getting briefed on the logistics, we were ready to face the beast that we had feared daily for the last year of our lives. When I left Jorge Luis on the operating table, the concept of good-bye never spoke to me more. Despite my fears, I kept reminding myself that this surgery could be the ticket to our son's ability to be normal. Every time I had a dark or scary thought about the surgery, I would tell myself that the surgery had the power to save our son's life. I had to force myself to accept the idea that the surgery could actually be a blessing and not a curse. I would repeat to myself that because of the procedure, Jorge Luis would also not have to bear the brunt of teasing from other kids at school, that he would be able to walk freely in the streets without being stared at. That moment, painful as it was to swallow, could mean everything for our son, so despite the challenge of leaving him in that hospital, we were resolved to do what was right for him.

Thankfully, the hospital was gracious enough to give us an early slot, and Jorge Luis was the first one on deck for what would be his first surgical procedure. Joe Torre was also kind enough to give Jorge the day off on the day of the surgery—which we were grateful for, considering that the All-Star Game was just around the corner.

After I left Jorge Luis in the hands of the surgeons Jorge and I decided that waiting around in the hospital was not going to do anyone any good. The plan was to go back to our apartment and wait the time out there, since at least there we could be comfortable and have some privacy. My parents, Jorge's father, Jorge, and I sat around, trying to drink our coffees and keep it light, checking our cell phones and watches and of course on one another. Jorge knew that he needed to stay strong for my sake.

I remember my mother doing crossword puzzles and Jorge talking with his father and pretending he was interested in reading the newspaper. I was emotionally paralyzed. I sat on the bed staring up at the ceiling, waiting for the hours to pass, waiting for the phone to ring, waiting to hear that my baby was still alive. I know it sounds awful, but I was honestly considering the possibility that our son was going to die. I just could not understand how a baby could survive something as gruesome as the surgery that had been described to me. Even for an adult I found it hard to imagine what it would be like. Every time the phone rang, my heart would drop and those nagging questions would come back: What did I do wrong? Did I drink something during my pregnancy before I knew I was pregnant? Did I eat the wrong foods? Did I not rest enough? Did I exercise too much? Did I have too many negative thoughts? Did I party too much when I was younger? Was there something I missed, something I forgot to do? The questions marched around in my mind for the entire time of my son's surgery, making me feel more vulnerable, more afraid, and more delicate than I had ever thought I could be. The grueling wait made me finally understand the essence of the human condition—one based on unremitting love and the sense of helplessness that inevitably comes with it.

The surgery occurred in various phases, each one involving a different doctor. First the anesthesiologist went in, followed by the pediatric neurosurgeon, Dr. Howard Weiner. Then Dr. McCarthy, the craniofacial surgeon, arrived and began the actual procedure. The life of my son was now in the hands of those individuals and their team of nurses, a gaggle of strangers whom I had no choice but to trust. For the next eleven hours, nurses from the hospital called us every time a new doctor came in and reported everything that had occurred with the previous one. Things seemed to be going well, and an hour before the surgery was finished, they called us once again, telling us to come back to the hospital, where we could wait for our son in the recovery unit. After we arrived, doctors and nurses came out and told us that the surgery had gone well, but nobody really explained what that meant. They were reserved and matter-of-fact in their explanations, making it all still feel so incredibly vague. We asked a million questions, but not one of their answers seemed to clarify any of it for us. I guess the doctors were weary of saying too much too soon, knowing that with a condition such as this one, the variables tend to shift without a moment's notice. They seemed to be relieved that this first major hurdle was behind us, and we would have to give it some time before they could inform us of what needed to happen next. It was terrible to be so utterly helpless regarding our own child, and all we could really do was pray that everything had gone well.

CHAPTER 17

Patience, Pain, and the Power of Unpredictability

Before you can inspire with emotion, you must be swamped with it yourself. Before you can move their tears, your own must flow.

—WINSTON CHURCHILL

Jorge:

When we came into the recovery room, we saw our son with his head tightly wrapped with a turbanlike bandage. We wondered if he could breathe, let alone see. His little eyes were swollen, and he could barely move. It is the cruelest of punishments to have to see one's child this way, a traumatic image that has the power to haunt a man forever. We spent the night there in the recovery room, sleeping upright in chairs beside our little survivor. Two days later we were transferred to the ICU, where the doctors kept a close watch on one of his eyes, which they wanted to make sure would open properly. They were also monitoring him to ensure that he did not have a fever, because that could indicate some kind of infection.

Laura spent every minute by Jorge Luis's side, from room to room, confidently marching right up to every doctor and every nurse who touched him. She was determined to always accompany him and to be his advocate, no matter her own fears about everything that was happening. We didn't have many visitors because at that point no one really knew too much about what was going on. We wanted that delicate moment to be all about our family and our ability to overcome this extremely challenging moment.

Manuel Mendez (Laura's brother):

I was in the ICU, and I remember little Jorge was all bandaged up and couldn't open his eyes. But when Laura entered the room and he heard her voice, you saw this genuine little smile start to form on his face. That exact moment that he heard the sound of his mother's voice, he knew that everything was going to be okay. He was so strong. I remember thinking that if this kid can survive this, anything is possible.

After three days when he opened his eye, we could finally go home. But for those three days he was so frustrated; you could tell he couldn't see very well, which made him incredibly irritable. All we could do was caress his little hands and talk softly to him. And of course, there was always his music. Somehow, the sound of music, even after the trauma he had just endured, would always calm him and bring him back to some kind of tranquillity. We like to think that the music acted as a gentle reminder for him to take in all of the beauty of the world, even in the worst of times. The music was his balm. We would assure him with the sounds that we played for him, along with the warm sensations of our touch, that his mom and dad would always be there to comfort him.

The doctors explained to us that the surgery had gone well, with no surprises to speak of, but that we would have to wait and see about the long-term aftermath because these cases tend to be extremely fluid. They helped us digest the critical idea that in any scenario of craniosynostosis, things occur not only in three dimensions, but actually in four, with this fourth dimension being time. They explained that with time, secondary changes in head shape can arise and become more severe, making the correction much more difficult.

But I started to feel a bit of relief for the first time since the onset of the ordeal, imagining that the worst part was at least starting to be over. During the surgery we met a lovely nurse who gave Jorge Luis a Barney doll that sang the infamous "I love you" song, which Jorge Luis completely adored. We ended up befriending the nurse, and fortunately for us, one of her friends at the time was a man named Edgar Andino, who became one of our best friends and has remained so to this day. Not only would he become our true pal, but in time he (along with myself and Laura's mother) would also donate blood to our son on a number of occasions.

I vividly remember the day when Jorge Luis's eyes fluttered open for the first time after the surgery. It was right before the game on a Sunday afternoon, and the moment I saw those sweet brown eyes look up at me, it felt as though the world had gone from shades of gray to a brilliant full-color display of possibilities. I went to the stadium with renewed energy and had a great game; I think I had six or seven RBIs that game. In fact, I managed to play one of the best games of my life, batting like a champ and catching with unwavering precision. Before that, I would fight with the umpires and sulk around with my stress written all over my face. I would try with all my might to be there for my pitchers, but it was a real challenge knowing my son would have to endure such serious measures and that somehow or other, his life was always on the line. Now that he had passed this first monumental challenge, my mind and body could be back on the field. It honestly felt as if our prayers had been answered, and it seemed that we could finally relax now that our boy had survived the worst.

Our doctors suggested that we let things be for one year and then see if the surgery had the right outcome, at which

Tino Martinez (fellow New York Yankee):

> *O*ne afternoon a group of us stopped at the hospital to see Jorge and Laura. We walked into that room and saw little Jorge all bandaged up, Laura's eyes red from crying and lack of sleep, and Jorge looking pretty much stunned. You knew right then, watching the scene, that life off the ball field was not easy for the Posada family. Somehow, still, they held their grace. It was inspiring.

point they could determine if he would require any further corrections. They explained that they did not want to do too much while he was so young, because the body grows and changes, so they had held back a bit during the initial operation. So we left the hospital knowing that the procedure had gone well but not knowing if it would be his last. We would have to wait *a whole year,* gradually easing into what would become a permanent wait-and-see scenario. Going into it, we had known that that was the case, but we were not prepared for the reality of it.

For the next few months we had to travel back and forth between New York and Puerto Rico according to my playing season, and we carefully watched our son as he healed from the surgery. He had a row of staples across his entire head in a zigzag shape, which they do to make the scar as discreet as possible. We covered his head with little Harley-Davidson scarves so that he wouldn't touch the wound. We were also instructed to give him antibiotics and to keep the doctors posted on any developments. As the months trickled along, his wound began to heal and the swelling started to go down. His face even looked more aligned, and the shape of his head appeared to be more even. We were actually starting to feel optimistic. We tried to make our son feel as normal as possible and watched him closely every day to see if things changed. We knew that we had to brace ourselves for the possibility of anything, but we were hopeful that the surgery had been effective.

But much to our dismay, in the spring of 2001 the peculiar deformation on the right front side of Jorge Luis's head came

Jane Mendez (Laura's sister):

I remember we went to eat at a Hispanic restaurant in the Bronx one afternoon, and this man said to Laura, "You know, your son's head doesn't look right." Laura calmly looked the guy dead in the eye and replied, "Thank you, sir, but he actually has a condition that does not allow him to hold his head straight. Thanks for your concern, but kindly mind your own business." Though the comments of people like this man were usually well intentioned, it was just one of those things that could make you crazy. My sister and Jorge had enough on their plates without the rest of the world feeling like they had to chime in, too.

Tino Martinez (fellow New York Yankee): ──────

> *A*t the All-Star Game, you're playing with the best players and are actually being recognized by the fans who voted for you. It is very much an honor and something you definitely want to achieve as a player, and you don't know how many times you'll have the opportunity to do it, because there are so many great players in the league. Every year one guy has a better year than another guy, so you really don't know when your last All-Star Game will be. So when you get a chance to play like Jorge did, you take full advantage. But he did a pretty good job of hiding his emotions.

back, and with it the realization that we were not going to be let off the hook that easily. A second surgery was scheduled for the following August, which confirmed the notion that moving forward, this was going to be our life. The fact is that Dr. McCarthy had warned us about the unpredictable nature of the illness and about the fact that facial features do, in fact, develop and shift at this stage of a baby's life. So despite the horror of knowing that the doctors would have to go back into Jorge Luis's head, at least now that we had been through one surgery, we knew what to expect. Regardless, the uncertainty of the whole thing was maddening.

That year I was chosen to play for the American League in the All-Star Game, which was a pretty big deal. The All-Star

Game is traditionally not just a "best of the best" play-off; more than that, it's a day dedicated to family and fun, a day of sportsmanship and camaraderie—everything that fathers and sons are all about. So you can imagine how I felt that day in July when the players were introduced and all of the fathers among them proudly ran out on the field along with their kids by their sides. I was the only father there whose kid couldn't accompany me out onto the field, and there was absolutely nothing that I could do to change that. I ran out there with a forced smile on my face, trying with all my strength to hide the wound in my heart.

PART V

Living with Endurance

Being deeply loved by someone gives you strength,
while loving someone deeply gives you courage.
—LAO TZU (CHINESE TAOIST PHILOSOPHER)

CHAPTER 18

Lessons in Fortitude

Laura:

We tried to remain optimistic, patiently waiting for the next August to come around again. When it finally did, Jorge Luis was twenty-one months old and ready to undergo his second surgery. He would again be in the hands of Dr. McCarthy, with the purpose of touching up what the doctor had done during the first procedure and to address any new deformations that might have developed throughout the course of the year. This year of waiting gave us ample time to further research the disease, and to become more acquainted with its treatment. We now understood that there was no easy answer or solution and that the treatment would be part of a moment-to-moment plan of attack.

The second surgery took place with no unforeseen complications, and this time around, since we kind of knew what to expect, we went into it with more confidence and less anxiety. Jorge Luis was discharged, and we were free to head home and carry on as best we could. Now we had a better sense of what the recovery would entail and the baby was a bit older and sturdier, so we had high hopes for his continued progress. Because everything felt more or less in control, Jorge thought it would be okay to go back on the road with the team. Things seemed to move along smoothly, until I realized a few days after the surgery, when the baby and I were back at home, that his head and eyes were still very swollen. Not only that, but he was also running a terribly high fever and crying uncontrollably all over again. He would wail hysterically all through the night, cries that were reminiscent of the early days of his diagnosis, which of course made me think that he was in excruciating pain. Between the fever, which wouldn't go down, and the swelling of his eyes, which seemed to get worse and worse, I was at a loss. After his first surgery, yes, we had seen some swelling, but this was something else. My instincts told me that something had definitely gone wrong, but there was nothing that I could do to understand what it was, and worse, I had no clue as to how to make him feel better. All I could think was that no baby should have to endure so much pain and hardship, and I felt guilty for not being able to bring him some comfort.

At one point, after being awake with Jorge Luis for more than thirty hours of nonstop crying while my husband was away, I could clearly see that the left side of his forehead looked tremendously red and irritated and was puffed out to the size of a tennis ball. I didn't like to bother my husband while he was on the road and remained resolved to handle even the most catastrophic situations on my own. Instead, in hysterics I called the doctors, who tried to calm me down by saying that a little fever was totally normal and that I should just give the baby some Tylenol. I was beside myself with exhaustion and agony for my little boy and thought that maybe some fresh air would do us both some good. I decided to take him out for a walk. When I hit the corner of Second Avenue and 86th Street, with Jorge Luis crying in my arms, a man started yelling at me, accusing me of child abuse and pointing to the side of my baby's forehead, which by this point looked downright scary, with his left eye almost entirely closed by the inflammation.

I ran upstairs into the house in tears, grabbed my purse, and took Jorge Luis back to his pediatrician for some real answers. Upon seeing the condition of the baby, the pediatrician immediately called Dr. McCarthy's office and explained the situation, whereupon they both finally agreed that I should take my son back to the hospital.

There I was met with a slew of befuddled doctors who had no idea what to make of our son's presenting condition. They looked at one another and at Jorge Luis with expressions of concern on their faces, but they did not say much. They could not give me the answers that I was looking for because, frankly, they had no idea what had gone wrong.

I vividly remember that when we arrived at the hospital something peculiar happened. I was assigned a room for Jorge

Luis, and when he saw the steel crib in that room he literally let go of me. That was something he had never done before and seemed to be his way of asking that I lay him down in the bed. It was as if he was finally surrendering, somehow knowing that he belonged in the care of doctors and experts.

The doctors began a flurry of tests to try to determine what was causing the fever and inflammation, but none of the results showed anything conclusive. They performed a CAT scan, and he was taken back into the operating room for further exploration of the wound, debridement (the removal of dead, damaged, or infected tissue to improve the healing potential of the remaining healthy tissue), and placement of drains and a subcutaneous irrigating system. They also performed a lumbar puncture, commonly known as a spinal tap, but still they could not figure out what went wrong. By now I was not only livid at the lack of clarity regarding my son's quickly worsening condition, but I was also completely heartbroken as I watched him endure test after painful test, totally at the mercy of his illness, the surgery, and now this mysterious complication that no one seemed to understand.

I was at last referred to a specialist on infectious diseases, who determined that Jorge Luis had an infection that was the result of bacteria known as peptostreptococcus and eikenella from his mouth that had entered the wound during the course of the recent surgery. By now my frustration and anger were really visible, and I knew that I was soon going to reach my emotional

limit. I was told that this type of infection could happen to anyone but that it was rare (a 3 percent chance). I took their word
for it because I had no other choice, but I was definitely shaken
by the new turn of events. I had lost a bit of faith and in doing so
came to realize that I would have to keep an even closer watch
on my son during every second of any hospital stay. I wanted
desperately to trust the medical community and to trust in God;
but after that debacle, I was shattered and enraged.

———————————

We were into and out of the hospital for six weeks before that
infection was finally resolved. During that time, one morning
I woke up in the hospital and, seeing my son sound asleep, I
thought, Perfect, I'll let him rest and go home for a quick shower.
It had been another one of those nights spent asleep in a hospital
chair. I was due for a walk outside, needed to freshen up, and,
though I never wanted to leave my son's side, let myself go home
for a shower that morning, knowing that my mother and Jorge
would stay in the hospital with the baby.

It was a beautiful morning, with clean, crisp fall air and a
bright blue sky that was nourishment for my soul. I was home
getting myself together when the phone rang, and on the other
end of the line was my husband, sounding as serious as I have
ever heard him, hurriedly instructing me to turn on the television. When I clicked the remote control, I saw the World Trade

Center blazing in a massive fire, black smoke billowing out into the sky, and the towers slowly crumbling down into a giant burning pile of dust. I didn't understand exactly what was happening to New York or what was happening in the world, for that matter, but I knew that I wanted my son to see my face when he woke up in this mayhem. Jorge and I mutually tried to calm each other down, and I assured him that I would get to the hospital as soon as possible. Little did I know what was waiting for me out on the streets . . .

I threw on a backpack, sprinted downstairs, and started to make my way downtown toward 34th Street, while everyone else on the island of Manhattan ran hysterically in the opposite direction. I saw terrified people huddled in circles holding one another, trembling and crying. A harried cacophony of sirens filled the air, while people madly rushed into and out of buildings, many of the faces, young and old, bearing empty, broken expressions. The looks in the eyes of the cops and firemen wrangling the masses told me that something terrible was transpiring. They seemed helpless and confused, trying to no avail to contain the frightened, clueless swarms of people. I heard mothers frantically calling the names of their children and saw business owners leaving their shops and stores hurriedly, everyone running from the hell that was raging in the financial district. Some of the people running uptown were covered in white soot, fleeing like traumatized specters from the worst thing they had ever encountered. I heard news coverage coming from taxi car radios, all of it muffled but serious-sounding, including reports of missing people and death counts. There was a lot of screaming, crying, and running—a whirlwind of panic that seemed to grab the city by its core. I still was not clear about what exactly had happened, but I knew that it was something monstrous and infinitely more catastrophic than any of us could even begin to imagine.

Sprinting down those New York City streets, all I could think about was seeing my son. But the cell phones were down, and I couldn't communicate with my husband, so there was a hysterical sense of being trapped alone in a cyclone of chaos. Everything felt apocalyptic. I argued ferociously with cops, sneaked weasel-like past barricaded streets, wriggled through terrified crowds, and somehow hustled my way down to the hospital. People thought I was insane for running toward Ground Zero, but as the rest of Manhattan did its best to survive, I had to see Jorge Luis.

When I arrived at the hospital I practically threw myself on to my baby's bed and held him close, fighting back tears of joy and relief. I didn't even have time or energy to process the fact that our city was essentially under siege and that the world as we knew it had fundamentally changed—all I cared about was the fact that my family was alive and together.

The terrorist nightmare simmered steadily for days and weeks, all of New York turned on its head, desperate to start the process of healing. Everyone stayed glued to their televisions, listening as Mayor Rudolph Giuliani tried to console a city that had just suffered the most tremendous loss imaginable. As for us, we stayed glued to our son's side, praying that he would also finally start to heal. We imagined that the hospital would be flooded with victims of the attack, but few came, as most of the wounded had already perished in the atrocity that had taken place. Jorge and I didn't want to be apart after the disaster and spent countless nights sleeping in makeshift beds or hospital cots by our son's side. I would even climb right into the crib with him on many of those nights. I never wanted him to have the feeling that his mama was anywhere but right by his side.

I remember there was a very sick little baby in the next room whom we would see every day with his mother. I never found out exactly what was wrong with the child, but it was evidently serious, and I felt a special sense of compassion toward the mother, who, like me, was trying to survive emotionally under some very traumatic circumstances. As a gesture of goodwill, I finally decided to go to the hospital shop downstairs and buy a teddy bear for the baby and perhaps make friends with the mom. I thought that we could bond over our pain and that maybe she would be someone who could understand me . . . but when I walked into the room that day, the baby had already passed away and the mother was gone. There was a dark stillness in that space that on the one hand struck me with a deep sadness and on the other hand forced me to count my blessings, as difficult as they were to see. Everything just seemed to go from bad to worse with every moment that passed, and the light that we thought we had seen at the end of the tunnel was now blackness with no end in sight.

After six weeks in the hospital and the crisis in New York as a highlight of the stay, we felt we could not take one more night. The world had been suddenly struck with the unforeseen tragedy of 9/11, while we simultaneously felt that we were in the throes of our own personal 9/11, a calamity that would only worsen with time, constantly testing our emotional limits and our ability to endure. We watched as the world began the harrowing process of mourning the epic loss of so many; we felt the collective devastation and silently feared for the life of our own son, who was untouched by the terrorist attack that occurred downtown but who was being assaulted by an entirely different breed of terror.

That was it: we had finally hit rock bottom.

CHAPTER 19

Square One

Jorge:

We sat in the hospital, which by now had become our second home, waiting in sadness and helplessness over everything that was transpiring in the world around us and, of course, within our own personal world. It felt like a downward spiral like no other, and what we were up against now made the early days of first hearing about the diagnosis seem like a walk in the park.

After much testing and deliberation, our doctors finally sat us down—with that wary look in their eyes that people always seem to have when they're on the brink of delivering a piece of bad news—and told us the brutal truth of what was coming next: our son would require at least *two more* surgeries. The first surgery would be to remove what the doctors had just placed in his cranium and clean the site of the infection thoroughly, whereupon we would have to wait for another entire year to then try a second surgery to redo the corrections all over again. Despite the hard work and diligence of our medical team, the last surgery had been a wash, as sometimes happens. Not only were we essentially right back at square one but now we also had two more surgeries looming in our ever-darkening horizon. There was nothing that I could do or say to make the situation better for Laura or Jorge Luis, and the doctors' conclusion and new plan for moving forward left a gaping hole of pain in the center of my heart. I kept asking myself, "How much more can we endure?"

For the next six weeks, the doctors tried all kinds of antibiotics to treat the infection until it was finally resolved. Now that his tubes were out, we could take him home, where Laura would give him antibiotics intravenously. She would remove the piece attached to his catheter (an intravenous tube), flush it with saline so that the line wouldn't close, insert the meds into the tube for half an hour, clean it, and flush it again. She did that twice a day for two weeks, and because she was also instructed not to wet his wound, she bathed him with washcloths for about three weeks. Just when I had thought my wife was on the brink of totally crumbling, she showed her true colors again by stepping up and taking charge with total confidence and assertion. It was as if she now considered herself an active participant on our son's medical team, and she took it upon herself to tend to him like a true professional. She was unstoppable, and if handling those obligations was at all difficult, she never once winced or showed weakness. She was like a lioness, undeterred, intent on protecting the well-being of her little cub. During that time I remember Laura actually climbing into Jorge Luis's crib and sleeping with him through the night. She just didn't want him to suffer or ever feel that he was alone, and she was petrified that he would pull out the line while sleeping and possibly bleed to death.

By now our concept of time was shattered, because we felt that we were always in a permanent state of waiting and seeing, like living life in a snow globe where the snow never actually settles and stills and question marks pop up like little demons with every turn and every choice. We seemed to be in some kind of surgery loop now, where the solution to every problem seemed to be another surgery, yet every surgery seemed to be the cause of the next problem.

We decided that after the mayhem in Manhattan and the fact that I am so well known there, maybe it was time to look for a surgeon outside of New York, where things might feel a bit more relaxed and where we could be more anonymous and private about our situation. The hustle of the city had run us ragged, and we were ready to take on the next leg of this journey with a bit more tranquillity. Dr. McCarthy understood our concerns and was unceasingly helpful and gracious in making sure that whomever would take on the case of our son would be adequately armed with all of the necessary information and details of his medical history.

After much research with the help of Luis Espinel, my

then agent and Laura's good friend from law school, we discovered Dr. Gerald Tuite, a well-reputed neurosurgeon, based in St. Petersburg. This was ideal because I would be in spring training there, so we could all be in one place together as we dealt with the surgery. Through Dr. Tuite, we were also referred to his colleague, a plastic surgeon, Dr. Ernesto Ruas, and it was decided that Jorge Luis's third surgery would take place in Florida.

Dr. Ruas was Latino, so right off the bat we felt that we could more easily communicate with him. He was a realistic guy who told us that he would do his best but that he could not make any promises. He made us see that we would have to face the fact that our son might never be perfect. But he also showed us that there was definitely hope for great improvement.

His meticulous process would include taking an MRI of Jorge Luis's head and molding an exact model of his skull, which would later be used during the surgery as a reference tool as the surgeons did the work. Drs. Tuite and Ruas determined that the postoperative infection that had occurred in New York had left Jorge Luis with cranial defects on the forehead, as well as ptosis—an abnormally low position of the upper eyelid—that would also require repair. They explained to us that Jorge Luis presented with loss of bone support over a large part of his face. Over his left forehead, they told us, there were missing bones, and large cranial bone defects along the front left side of his head. They also pointed out that he showed a visible head tilt. They spoke another flurry of words that we did not understand

and described problems that we did not know how to solve, and though we felt that things could not possibly get any worse than the last debacle, we were still extremely nervous not only because of the surgery itself but because of the risk of another infection. We swallowed hard, tried as best as we could to shelve our fears, and put our trust in the hands of these new doctors, hoping and praying that this time things would go well.

Laura and I felt infinitely calmer knowing that we would be away from the bustle and pressure of the city, and hopeful in the face of this new plan. And despite the agony of our extended hospital stays and the trauma of 9/11, we were ready to move forward in the treatment of our son. But just as we were packing up to head to Florida, we had yet another surprise: Laura was pregnant again.

CHAPTER 20

Old Fears,
New Fears

Laura:

The news of my pregnancy came with a mix of emotions for all of us. On the one hand, we knew that we definitely wanted to have more children, but you can imagine that after what we were going through with Jorge Luis, the prospect of having another sick child felt like some kind of cruel joke. We were monumentally torn: though we already loved this new baby who was growing in my belly by the moment, we simultaneously feared for her little life—a paradox that gave a whole new dimension to the serious issues we were already navigating. Even though we knew that our son's case was not genetic, we could not fathom having to endure this uncertainty all over again and, even worse, having to watch yet another child suffer.

I cried throughout the entire pregnancy, agonizing over the

possibilities. Try as I might to resist letting my imagination get the best of me, I would wake up in the middle of the night, shooting straight up out of bed in a cold sweat, recovering from some horrendous nightmare about a baby born without an arm or a leg. From morning to night I would be disturbed by horrendous visions of my potentially sick baby number two, involuntarily torturing myself with details about the awful, unforeseeable possibilities. I felt guilty for having fears about a life that had not even yet begun and even guiltier for being the one to bring that life into the world.

Jorge found it challenging to communicate with me during this pregnancy, as I was often in the foulest of moods. I would cry and have tantrums, both of which Jorge understood were a result of the hormones and the fear. He knew it was hard for me because we were living between New York and Tampa, where I didn't have many friends, and our house in Florida was a temporary rental while we waited for our real home to be finished. This was all during spring training, which meant that Jorge had to be up and out of the house every morning by 6 A.M., so I was left alone a lot. We didn't have a babysitter, a nanny, or a maid, and everything was in as much a state of flux as it could be. Looking back, I probably resented Jorge (even slightly or unconsciously) since I was always the one contending with our son's doctors and appointments, and now I was also the one who was pregnant with our daughter. He still had the luxury of going out and doing what he loved most, which often left me feeling as if I were the one carrying the heavier load.

Thankfully, I received some relief when my old friend from law school, Luis Espinel, decided to move in with us for a while to keep me company and help out around the house. Not only did he single-handedly help us to find our new medical team for Jorge Luis, but he was also, much to my husband's relief, one of the only people in the world who could quickly bring a smile to my face.

But I was petrified about my growing baby. Every time I went to the doctor, I would ask a million questions, pleading for sonograms and demanding to know if the shape of the baby's head looked all right. I am sure the doctors viewed me as completely paranoid, but I could not control the anxiety that kept growing along with my belly. I was obsessed, of course, with good reason. The gamble was on, and we really had absolutely no clue as to what we were in for.

But to all of our delight, our little blessing of a daughter, Paulina, was born perfectly healthy on July 15, 2002, and her arrival brought a little piece of unexpected sunshine into all of our lives. When we saw her with all ten fingers and toes, smiling bubbly up at us, we were struck with a massive gush of total gratitude. Our little girl was healthy and beautiful, and for that moment we were reminded of what true joy feels like. Neither of us will ever forget what we felt the day our girl came into the world: it was a blend of appreciation, love, happiness, and relief (and maybe a bit of sadness for Jorge Luis, who now had the task of growing up with a perfectly healthy little sister). However, ever the loving soul, Jorge Luis came into the delivery room that day with his arms full of presents for the newest member of our family—and they have been buddies ever since.

It was just Jorge and I at Paulina's birth, and I could tell that we both felt as though our love had been accentuated by this spectacular miracle. If the difficult chapter of dealing with our son's diagnosis was running us ragged, the birth of our daughter revitalized us, reminding us that the process of cultivating a family was only just beginning. Paulina basically brought us back to life, making us realize that we would always have the duty of being the best parents possible, no matter what the odds against us. Though she was born perfectly healthy, she was still a baby, *our baby,* and would require our presence regarding all the details of her existence. She would be as dependent on us as her older brother, and, despite her good health, we were intent on making sure that she would get all the attention that she ever needed.

Even after Paulina was born, when she was still a little baby, I would routinely ask Jorge to check on her to see if she was developing okay, if she was breathing, and to make sure there were no new surprises. There was definitely an element of fear, even paranoia, as we watched our new little one grow. Fortunately we were given a respite, as not only would Paulina turn out perfectly healthy, but she would also turn out to be the family jester, providing comic relief at every given opportunity. Even when she was a little baby, she never cried. She was always smiling, she ate well, and she seldom got sick. She was a perfect, problem-less little angel. Each day she evolved into an even funnier version of herself, cracking us up with her wild antics and reminding us always to look for that proverbial silver lining.

Imagine this scene: we were sitting in the living room one day talking about something serious, when from her room emerged a totally rocked-out Paulina, toy electric guitar in tow, playing with a Hendrix-like scowl on her face. From the day she was born, she was a one-woman show, a tiny diva who would snag center stage with abandon. She was always so passionate, completely engaged with the world around her, and she consistently makes us smile. It was almost as if she always knew that it was her job to help us through.

We were now fortunate to have some help too, so thankfully, we could also continue to focus on helping Jorge Luis. It was a tricky balance to keep, because we knew it was important for Paulina to have present, attentive parents too. Remember, she was born into a family in the midst of serious turmoil, so she needed just as much support, care, and guidance as the rest of us.

———————

The next months moved along gingerly with the excitement of our new baby, and we waited in anticipation for Jorge Luis's next surgery, which was slated for February 18, 2003. Now that he was a bit older and moving into toddlerhood, it appeared that he was starting to somehow identify with his situation a bit better. He would look in the mirror knowingly, seeming to understand that his scar had to have come from somewhere. As his parents, we harbored all kinds of anxieties about how we would one day fully explain his disease to him, how we would find the courage to be completely honest with him about what life had doled out to him. We also feared that he would begin to feel bad about himself, with his healthy new little sister now thrown into the mix.

Moreover, Jorge and I felt strongly about the fact that we didn't want our son to wake up in the hospital with a monumental headache and not have a clue in the world as to why. We felt it was our duty as his parents to tell him the truth. We didn't want him to think, "Why did my mom and dad do this to me?" He would forever remember us being the ones who had put him down on those sterile hospital beds, so at the very least we felt we owed him a good reason. We like to believe that when you are dealing with children, the best policy is to be completely honest, using words and ideas that are basic and not scary.

The night before the surgery in Tampa, I sat with Jorge Luis in the evening and said, "Sweetie, tomorrow you are going to have an operation that's going to make you better, because you were born with a problem in your head. It's going to be like a puzzle that the doctors are going to put together." I told him that it might hurt a bit, but I also promised that it was going to make him stronger and healthier and that we were 100 percent certain that it was the right choice to make. I assured him that Mami and Papi had chosen the best doctors in the best hospitals, that we would be with him the whole time, and that in a few days he would be all better. I was adamantly positive with him, perhaps because I instinctively felt that the power of my conviction could help him endure such a critical and precarious moment of his life. He just looked up at me and said, "Okay, Mama," not even knowing what he was agreeing to but clearly grateful that we'd had the chat. He never once showed fear and always nobly accepted every twist and turn that came his way. In fact, it was his strength that fed my ability to get through each moment and his adultlike equanimity that inspired me to stay calm. He seemed like an old soul who instinctively knew that life came with pain, and he came across as totally poised and unafraid to face whatever came his way.

CHAPTER 21

Halos and Heroes

God who sends the wound sends the medicine.
—MIGUEL DE CERVANTES SAAVEDRA

Jorge:

O n February 18, 2003, Jorge Luis was admitted to All Children's Hospital in St. Petersburg for what would be his third major surgery to repair the defects in his skull from the botched second surgery. Once again he underwent a reconstruction of his forehead, and once again we were at the mercy of his elusive illness, which seemed to have a temperament all its own. By that point, all we could do was remain neutral: we didn't want to be too hopeful, at the risk of having our illusions shattered yet again—but we also wanted to show a certain degree of optimism and faith, which we knew could have the power to fuel the scenario with the right kinds of energy. It was a delicate balance that we needed to find, a balance that would allow us to accept, endure, and carry on with courage and dignity.

But beyond balance, it was love itself that always seemed to guide our way. I remember right before the surgery, after they sedated Jorge Luis and he slowly began to doze, he said to Laura, "I loooooove you, Mami," in the sweetest, most sincere daze either of has ever beheld. She could not stop laughing—and, well, crying, too. They really have always been like one soul. In Spanish we say, *"Uña y carne,"* which literally means "the flesh attached to a fingernail"—which is how close they really are. So even in that dark vortex of bad memories, there were some very special moments.

The doctors seemed pleased with the results of the operation, so we were, of course, overjoyed. When Jorge Luis finally awoke, he was totally alert, his wound seemed to be healing properly, he was eating and drinking with no problem, and, according to the doctors, he was also neurologically intact. Even his appearance seemed somewhat improved. Our fear of medicine, doctors, and surgeries began to transform into gratitude and appreciation for those valiant individuals who dedicate their lives to fixing people.

We were sent home three days later, feeling better than ever and ready to finally move on with our lives. After all that had happened and everything we had learned, we knew that we would always have to keep a close eye on our son's development, but at least by now we knew (to the degree that one *can* know)

what we were up against. We understood now that part of dealing with an illness such as craniosynostosis is to learn how to
embrace the uncertainty that it comes with and simultaneously
do our best under such indefinite conditions.

About a week after the surgery, there was a photograph taken of
Jorge Luis, smiling happily on his tricycle, wearing a little hat. It
was incredible; just one week after that elaborate procedure he
was up and about, playing, exploring, and finally having some
fun. We had a brand-new baby girl and a healthy, healing child,
and for the first time in ages, *everything was perfect.*

Throughout Jorge Luis's first few years, being so afraid of
neurological impairment or problems with his cognitive func-
tion, we became extremely conscious of teaching him things like
colors and numbers, always stimulating his curiosity and consistently feeding him new information and imagery. We planted
the seeds for his appetite to learn. Now feeling more comfortable about his appearance, we could also finally put him into
school, as the Florida doctors had done a good job of making his
condition slightly less obvious. He knew to avoid certain activities for safety, but we made every effort to let him live a normal
life. People would ask him about his scar and he was always open
and honest about it, more grown up than any of us might have
been. When I really think about it, Jorge Luis *always* behaved

like a little adult, poised, sturdy, and ready to take on whatever needed to happen. After all the various procedures and plans and all the curveballs and complications, we finally understood the fluid nature of his condition.

Fortunately for us, after years of bouncing from hospital to hospital, after the botched surgery with its ensuing complications, and after what seemed like an eternity of trying to keep up with a disease that morphs as it pleases with the passage of time, we serendipitously encountered yet another doctor. This one, however, would ultimately become our all-around mentor, support system, and trusted answerer of questions regarding all matters of the disease. The esteemed Dr. David Staffenberg would change the way we understood and dealt with craniosynostosis, stepping in as Jorge Luis's official doctor in 2006. In an auspicious moment, we were fortunate enough to meet him after being invited to the Children's Hospital at Montefiore in the Bronx, where we were visiting kids and delivering Christmas presents. It was a total blessing, and we like to believe that meeting this extraordinary man was, in turn, a Christmas present for us. Although the Florida surgery had gone relatively well, we learned through our new friend and doctor Dr. Staffenberg that there was room for even more improvement.

We knew that we would need a New York–based doctor to monitor Jorge Luis's development and were thrilled to be able to consult with Dr. Staffenberg, a true pioneer in the field of craniofacial reconstruction and an all-around lovely person. We

Dr. David Staffenberg:

*T*hink of every baby as a snowflake—no two are exactly alike. That said, each case of craniosynostosis is unique and has its own set of circumstances to deal with. But as with snowflakes, there are predictable patterns, and within each type, there are degrees of severity.

soon discovered that he was the renowned surgeon who separated the famous conjoined twins in 2004 and quickly learned about this young doctor's innovative vision and commitment to the field.

It is through his wisdom and talent that we could now, with confidence, face craniosynostosis head-on for the rest of our lives. We were much more relaxed by the time we were in his hands, having been through the worst of it already. We knew that, moving forward, we would be associated with a doctor whom we could trust blindly in all matters regarding our son's health and well-being. Dr. Staffenberg meticulously took the time to explain everything; he let us ask every question, and he even *anticipated* our questions, calmly explaining to us every possibility, keeping us in the loop of each decision being made. Given the fluidity of the disease, he said, he likes to see his patients every year until they are at least sixteen or seventeen, to make sure that all of the primary, secondary, and any other changes that arise can be dealt with and addressed by the time the patient reaches full physical maturity. Needless to say, we were in awe of his level of passion and uncontestable confidence in his work.

When we took Jorge Luis in for an initial consultation, Dr. Staffenberg explained to us that what made our son's case problematic was the fact of some very severe complications that had arisen as a result of the second surgery. He also explained that Jorge Luis might not have even required the second surgery if the first surgery had been successful and that the infection that had come about after that surgery had destroyed a significant portion of his skull, forcing the bone to then collapse back where it had come from. So by the time Dr. Staffenberg saw him after the multiple operations, he concluded that our son's appearance hadn't really improved much at all. He said that his scar was actually getting worse and that he was not holding his head up straight. He could also tell right away that Jorge Luis had scoliosis; and since part of his forehead was sunken in, he could also see that the bridge of his nose was deviated and pulling over in one direction. Though hearing this assessment was not exactly good news, we were thrilled at the fact that Dr. Staffenberg seemed to be looking at every sliver of every detail, leaving nothing unaccounted for and really assessing the potential improvement of our son from every possible angle known to him.

The surgical plan he presented to us included a complete revision of Jorge Luis's previous reconstruction; removal of the retained hardware; and reparation of the missing facial bone

Dr. Staffenberg:

*I*t is crucial to understand that when we assess any scenario of craniosynostosis, it does not only occur in three dimensions—but actually in *four,* with the fourth dimension being *time.* But fortunately, by anticipating and staying ahead of these types of problems, we can actually reverse this and manipulate the fourth dimension to work in our favor: instead of the deformation becoming worse and worse, with time our corrections will actually get better and better. This fourth dimension of time is unique to pediatric facial surgery because most surgeons are usually dealing with adult problems, where that fourth dimension does not exist because the patient has already reached full physical maturity. But with children, even if we can make something look great now, if it doesn't grow properly *in time,* then we are not doing the best we can.

In the case of Jorge Luis, had he not been treated properly, he would perhaps have a more pronounced tilt of the head, which leads to a tightening in the neck, which in turn, could lead to scoliosis and hip problems. Down the road, other problems can happen, and it really is all connected. For this reason, as far as kids go, that variable of the fourth dimension, time, is essential in *any* assessment and treatment of craniosynostosis.

using bone grafts from unaffected parts of his skull. He explained to us that resorbale (self-dissolving) hardware would be used for the bony fixation throughout and that at the end of the surgery, the scar would look much less pronounced. We chose to trust Dr. Staffenberg unconditionally and allow him to carry on with what sounded like a thoughtful and deliberate surgical strategy.

Of course our son always looked gorgeous to us, maybe because at a certain point we simply stopped looking for the imperfections. We really had no major complaints after the Florida surgery and before meeting our new doctor were already resolved to live with the results of that procedure. Still, everything that Dr. Staffenberg was now saying to us made sense, and we quickly realized that the doctor's critical assessment of our son's treatment thus far and his plan for future treatment could significantly improve his appearance, his health, and his life.

The doctor explained that despite the series of surgeries, Jorge Luis's synostosis (fusion of the cranial bones) was still there, and because it was still there, secondary growth problems were likely going to continue. If not dealt with in time, the deformations would gradually become more pronounced, which would throw us even deeper into the abyss that we had desperately been trying to crawl out of for years. Hearing Dr. Staffenberg lay it out for us this way made us quickly realize that if anyone held the key to a truly happy ending, it was very likely going to be he.

Dr. Staffenberg and his team operated on Jorge Luis in December 2006, when our son was six years old. The procedure was beyond successful, without complications, and Jorge Luis was discharged after three days. The morning after the surgery our little boy opened his eyes, which were all bandaged and swollen (a sight that we were by now accustomed to), and asked in the most poised manner you can imagine if he could please have a mirror so that he could look at his wound. Dr. Staffenberg told us that no other child had ever made such a request, that these young patients do not typically show such maturity in the face of such a painful and confusing ordeal. He seemed surprised to see our little man taking ownership of his reality with such grace and courage. He also told us that I was the only father he had ever encountered who asked to participate in the removal of his child's stitches. I guess I was compelled to do so because for the first time in ages, I felt that I had control over a situation that had at one point consumed me with total uncertainty. Removing my son's stitches felt somehow symbolic of removing his pain. Now the situation felt manageable to me, and my newfound relief empowered me with optimism, preparing me to take on whatever would come next.

This final surgery with Dr. Staffenberg was not something we had been expecting. However, when it came around we knew it was the logical next step in the flow of Jorge Luis's recovery. In time we would consider this final procedure the most successful one to date, a testament to the power of never giving up and the virtue in always looking for improvement. I remember sitting with Jorge Luis in the recovery room when he asked for the mirror. He looked at his reflection, turned to me, and said, "I look good." In that moment I knew that he understood.

CHAPTER 22

From Victims to Warriors

Adversity precedes growth.

—ROSEMARIE ROSSETTI

Laura:

R eflecting back on all those years of suffering, we cannot help thinking about some of the things that helped us to survive emotionally. At the top of that list, of course, were our family and friends, who were all there from the moment they each found out about what was going on. But going a bit deeper, what we believe really fueled our resilience was our profound realization that it was time to step outside of our own little worlds.

By the time our son was a little over a year old, we realized that the great secret of his illness was going to be something that we could hide from the world (not to mention our world) for only so long. Now that we had been through the critical hurdle of the first major surgery, we began to understand the fluctuating nature of the treatment for craniosynostosis. We also felt some kind of emotional shift: not only were we feeling more informed and ready to face off against the illness ourselves, but also, in that understanding, we came to realize that our experience could mean something more than just a case of bad luck for us. It became clear that within every single moment of what we had been through (and would continue to face), there was something to learn and, more important, something to impart.

Jorge and I gradually started to come to terms with the fact that we would have to start telling people about what was going on, but we were clear that we wanted to do it in an elegant way that had nothing to do with news and gossip (which we were afraid of, given Jorge's standing as a key player of the New York Yankees) and everything to do with human compassion. We reflected on the painful moments right before our son's various surgeries, realizing that perhaps, through such hardship, our pain could show us a new and improved plan for the present. Together, we looked long and hard at those somber moments of not knowing what was going to happen next and began to think of all the other people in the world who were up against similar situations. We imagined countless new moms and dads around the globe hearing the word "craniosynostosis" for the first time, consumed with dread, as we had been, at the prospect of what that could mean. We pictured those families shaking with fear the way we had, lost without answers, unsure what their future would bring. We envisioned the poor little beings born into the world, only to be immediately stamped with this horrible diagnosis, and their helpless parents, whose illusions were instantly smashed into a million little pieces. We thought of all the people who could not afford lifesaving surgeries, and of kids who would have to live with deformity as part of their very identity. Suddenly, we found ourselves commiserating with these families as if they were our flesh and blood and feeling their anguish as our very own. This sense of compassion went far beyond just *relating* to these individuals—at that point, we were determined to help them.

Jorge and I sat for hours and brainstormed about what we could do that would actually make a difference, something above and beyond simply donating money. We talked at length about how we could make the noblest use of our social status, wanting to come up with a mission that would make the welfare of craniosynostosis patients its utmost priority. We began to mutually envision a platform that could serve as an information forum for medical professionals and families alike, an entity that would both educate and support. It started to become clear that what we wanted to create was the very thing we were missing when first facing the disease ourselves. During those most difficult moments, we needed a resource that would arm us with all the information relevant to the disease, as well as the necessary emotional support to get through it. Through this realization, our new mission was starting to emerge, and with it a new road map of purpose.

At last, instead of being victims, we decided to become warriors. This meant that we would no longer sit idly wallowing in our own misery, simply allowing other families to feel the way we had for months on end. Despite our own pain and uncertainty, it was time to grow and open our hearts to all those families. Our situation was no longer just about us—it was now about everyone. As we began to accept our son's affliction and emotionally stepped outside the bounds of our nuclear family, we were able to consider every child born with craniosynostosis. In this new space of compassion, we could imagine their individual battles against the disease and think of creative ways that we could be of assistance.

Moving forward, we would begin to perceive our own struggle as a catalyst for something greater. Our experience could poise us to help other, perhaps less fortunate families to cope—emotionally *and* logistically—with this type of pain. We would show them that they too could find that proverbial light at the end of the tunnel, against all odds. With the help of our friend Luis, we ultimately decided to create the Jorge Posada Foundation, whose sole purpose would be to raise awareness of, disseminate education on, and provide resources to battle against the disease, and to offer whatever support we could to the patients and their families all along the way.

Though it was slightly daunting to know that we were at

last going to publicize what had been our personal nightmare, we held our heads high, looked the world dead in the eye, and, with all the courage we could muster, finally told our story. Despite the fear of an ensuing media frenzy and the horrible prospect of our son's facial deformations being front-page news in New York City, we held a formal press conference on November 1, 2000, where we explained the full story of our son's illness, his surgeries, and our decision to create the Jorge Posada Foundation. In a flash, we were able to turn something negative into a positive experience, thereby empowering our family and hopefully many others. It became clear that if we could continue to use whatever celebrity status we had to make a difference for people with the illness, some good might come from any pain we may have felt. Our personal mission was to move from selfish to selfless, taking the focus away from the details of our own suffering and instead homing in on the bigger picture of the illness and on what we could do to make a lasting difference.

For the first time in a long time, things started to make sense, and the act of publicizing our issue really allowed me to personally grow and change. We were finally able to shed our fears about what other people would think or say, how Jorge's fans would react, how the media would handle it. We simply didn't care anymore, as it was all about our family, our plan, and our new sense of purpose. We were focused inward in a way that we had never imagined possible, guided by the force of wanting to be positive in a world so laden with negatives. It started to become the only thing that really mattered. We were ready to continue confronting our son's illness with the knowledge that our help to other families would always give us strength. Being able to support other families in the same situation aids in the healing process and allows us to move forward.

———————

As part of our new agenda of advocacy, I became a board member of the National Foundation for Facial Reconstruction (NFFR), an organization that is the fund-raising arm of the Institute of Reconstructive Plastic Surgery (IRPS) at NYU Medical Center, headed by Dr. Joseph McCarthy. Working with Dr. McCarthy brought the experience full circle, as he was the one who, thankfully, diagnosed Jorge Luis when he was just ten days old, putting us on the path toward his eventual recovery. I was thrilled to be invited to be a board member and completely honored when I was voted in to collaborate with this amazing organization, which has helped thousands of patients from all over the world; plus it was a great opportunity for me to learn how a successful foundation is run.

Trickier to handle (though endlessly cute) has been our little daughter, Paulina, who, of course, was jealous of all of the attention that Jorge Luis always received and forever wondered why there was no foundation created in *her* name. She wondered why Jorge Luis's problems were so important and why everyone was always talking about him. Why was he always the center of attention, and where was the foundation for her? What was so special about him? For a while, seeing all the special interest Jorge Luis would receive, Paulina felt left out because she was healthy. She honestly believed that being sick was something positive and naively wished that she too could fall ill so that everyone would also make a big fuss over her. She felt completely left out, and it was not until we were in Hawaii on vacation, when she came down with a vile flu that set her vomiting her little soul out, that she understood clearly that being sick is not something good.

Still, it was our duty to provide her with as normal a life as we could. We wanted Paulina's childhood to be untainted by the heaviness of what we were facing, and her well-being became another variable to juggle in the ongoing craziness. We made it a point to designate special "Paulina Time," little activities designed to temper her rightful jealousy. These could include private excursions, just she and I, where we could focus on fun girly plans like shopping and manicures. When Jorge Luis was old enough to go to summer camp, Jorge and I even took Paulina on trips just for her, some of which would include a vacation in Disney World and another one in Anguilla. Though we didn't want to spoil her, we felt strongly about making sure that she would always feel just as special and loved as her brother.

One evening at a gala to benefit the foundation, little Paulina ran to the microphone and said, "Hi, my name is Paulina,

I'm Jorge's kid sister, and I don't have 'stosis, but I got hurt, too."
She had fallen when she was three years old and then required
stitches in her forehead. She was adorable in her effort to share
the stage with her brother, who by now was showing incredible
signs of improvement and a markedly better quality of life. The
future was starting to look sunny again, and we were at once
grateful, fulfilled, and determined to keep the fire of strength
burning. The path had been cleared, the worst part was over, and
our place in this world was newly defined.

PART VI

Onward and Upward

_____

Start by doing what's necessary; then do what's possible;
and suddenly you are doing the impossible.

—ST. FRANCIS OF ASSISI

CHAPTER 23

Share to Heal

Jorge:

We remember when our son was about to enter his first surgery and the untamable anxiety we felt from knowing what they were actually going to do to him. The description of the procedure sounded more like a torture method than a medical solution, and it was nearly impossible for us to accept the fact that something so invasive could actually help our son. We could not imagine how he would survive such a thing at just nine months and prayed ceaselessly until we knew that he had come through it.

The worst part was thinking that it would never be over. You trust that the doctors know what they are doing and that they will have solutions for everything that happens, and then you realize that some things are beyond the doctors and complications can arise at any moment. And just like that, you are back in the OR. Nobody wants to see his child go through that. You feel guilty about him not being able to do the things that other kids do and guilty that all you have been able to show him is the inside of a hospital room.

Though we knew the surgery was a necessary step, we somehow felt like the bad guys for being the ones to put him through it. In those days it often felt as if we were carrying our hearts around like 200-pound weights in our chests. We honestly believed that nothing and no one could bring us comfort in those moments, but in reality *we were sadly mistaken.*

If we could retrace those steps today, perhaps we would have been more open to the notion of speaking with other parents facing the illness and exchanging thoughts and ideas about what this difficult process is like. We were so busy stewing in our own anger, self-pity, and uncertainty that we blindly passed on the chance to communicate and potentially gain support from other families dealing with the problems and questions that craniosynostosis can bring up. We were obviously afraid of the media attention and the risk of becoming tabloid fodder, which might introduce our son in a negative light and make him prone to public mockery. Perhaps we were also scared of exposing ourselves, of showing our vulnerability; maybe we were going through good old-fashioned denial; or maybe we just didn't know how else to act. We should have instead remembered the saying "There is strength in numbers" and spent more time talking to people who have had experience with the disease firsthand. Had we taken the time and energy to seek, vent to, and exchange experiences with others in similar situations, we would have armed ourselves more thoroughly for the battle that lay ahead. Today, after everything that we have endured, we cannot say enough about the power of communication in the face of such personal, emotional hardship. Exchanging information with other families can help people to soften, to open up, and to really delve into all of the sensitive and logistical intricacies involved in coping with the disease. Talking not only gets us to express our feelings and challenges, it also gives us the chance to be active listeners, to show our support and our sense of understanding and, of course, give of our love. People need people, it is as simple as that, and the positive strength of a group enduring the same type of hardship can far outweigh the fear and pain that may come with the experience. People also need hope, and looking at everything that we went through and seeing that we survived is always an uplifting boost for all of the people we talk to.

During some of our most challenging moments, we looked for information in encyclopedias, in books, on the Internet, and on television, but somehow they were all dead ends. All we would find were medical explanations with chilling illustrations that did little to satisfy our need for concrete information. But looking back now, we can see that what we were really missing was hearing another mother or father tell us that everything was going to be okay.

We also came to understand that *knowledge* itself is just as essential when facing this (or any) disease. By raising awareness within the medical community and beyond, we can arm as many people as possible with the necessary information to confront this illness fully.

Granted, we are beyond grateful that most of Jorge Luis's surgeries have been successful and that we have been able to support all of his procedures financially. However, there are many families who are not as fortunate, who really cannot bear the financial brunt of one surgery (never mind eight). So one of the main purposes of the Jorge Posada Foundation is to reach out to families in need and not only to offer them emotional support through a special family support network but to also provide assistance to underwrite a portion of the costs of initial surgeries in its partner medical centers.

You have to consider that the costs for these types of procedures can become very intimidating to an in-need family, and the insurance, the copayments, and the deductibles can become exceedingly high, even if there are no complications. A typical craniosynostosis surgery can mean a hospital stay of anywhere from four days to two weeks. Health care is so expensive that it can leave an entire family bankrupt. Families who already have huge bills from just the birth of their child end up having to also finance these expensive surgeries that they never anticipated. To help keep the costs in check, the foundation steps in to negotiate with the hospital, and we really serve as an advocate for families, who are sad, scared, and vulnerable and often don't have the power to voice their concerns.

Through fund-raising efforts such as our yearly Heroes4Hope

Lisa Niederer (Jorge Posada Foundation Mentor):

*U*nfortunately, my son was diagnosed late, when he was already three years old. At that point, he underwent a reconstructive surgery and a new plate was placed into his head. In time, the plate dissolved but his bones didn't grow back properly. For the next few years he would have missing pieces of bone on the top of his head that the doctors would try to correct, each time to no avail.

We knew we were in need of one proper surgery to finally close the gap in our son's head and were stunned when we were told that our primary insurance company would not be covering the cost of such a surgery, claiming that this type of procedure is "elective" or "cosmetic" and demanding to know if our son had sustained some other injury that could explain his condition.

For three months we haggled with the insurance company, trying to educate it about craniosynostosis and desperately fighting for the cause of our son. Finally one day I marched over to their offices with CT scans of my son's skull in my purse and said, "Look, this is my son's skull—the way it is now, you can actually see his pulse through it. If you don't cover the cost of this surgery, he's going to go through life with this hole in his head. If it were your child, what would you do?"

We know that our son's late diagnosis did not help our case, which is why we now understand that the most important thing about this illness is to raise awareness so that doctors are less prone to miss the condition, one that requires a quick diagnosis and treatment in the first twelve months of a baby's life. In the end, we convinced the insurance company to pay for the surgery. Today we are proud mentors of the Jorge Posada Foundation and proud soldiers in the army of love they have created to confront this disease.

Gala, which takes place every year in New York, we use the opportunity to spread the word, raise money, and honor the families and doctors who are involved with our work. We invite and acknowledge various honorees or beneficiaries from the partner hospitals, but it is also open to the public. As we see it, this is an equal opportunity disease, and anyone who wants to learn about or support it will always have a seat at our table. The endeavor has become a full-circle experience, as it is through the hard work and tireless efforts of our good friend Edgar Andino—who not only donated blood to our son, but also stood with us in the darkest hours—that our fund-raising gala events have always been so successful.

We now know that we should have taken the opportunity to talk with parents going through the same thing when we first received our son's diagnosis. Trapped by our own fear and sadness, we didn't allow anyone else in. We pushed ourselves deeper into the abyss by not allowing the experiences of others to help guide us through the muck. This was a huge mistake on our part, a lesson that we now use as impetus and motivation for our agenda. Today, we encourage communication, because we understand that information is the key to tackling this illness. Through our foundation's unique mentorship program, families newly dealing with a diagnosis of craniosynostosis are linked with families who have already been down that road. In this way, the worldwide support system for craniosynostosis becomes fully empowered, providing all of us with every possible resource—emotional, logistical, or otherwise—to fully overcome the illness. We have amazing doctors who also serve as mentors, making themselves available right up to the surgery, even sending flowers and teddy bears to the families they treat and sticking around to guide them through the aftermath. After all, these are children we are talking about, and because craniosynostosis is a disease that is discovered in babies, the emotional element of the challenge becomes immense; as many parents will tell you, sometimes all it takes is the simple knowledge that someone else out there knows exactly how you feel. In our rockiest moments, we would remind ourselves that if we, grown adults, feel helpless, we have to remember that the poor baby is completely defenseless, a little creature who just needs someone to always be there with him, if only to caress him and embrace him with love. Even though we didn't know if everything was going to be okay, we needed our baby to know that he was loved and taken care of every single moment of his life. So we gave all of ourselves to our son and, in that process, surrendered ourselves entirely to his needs.

Now we also understand how much happiness you can give another parent with a simple glance, a few words of support, a hug, or just a call from a stranger living a parallel life. Today, we don't feel like wasting any more of our time asking "Why did this happen to us?" Now we feel that through the foundation, there are more important things we can do to help other children and families who are affected. To us, it has become crystal clear that "why" is not really the question to ask anymore, but instead "What can we do to help as many people as possible?" And this is precisely what informs and inspires our deepest beliefs and goals today.

Laura tells some of the mothers, "If you want to scream, scream; if you want to cry, cry; if you want to go silent, go silent—do whatever you have to do to vent your feelings." There are no right or wrong reactions. Just let yourself feel what you feel; though the condition is very scary, the good news is that there is always hope for treatment and full recovery. Let hope be like your breath, fueling you with everything you need to get through those most difficult times.

It is said that everything is 20/20 in hindsight, a cliché that is incredibly true for us as we reflect on the question of how we would have done things differently. We were so locked into our own agony that perhaps we lost sight of some fundamental truths. Of course, there is no sense in beating ourselves up for the things we did not do or did wrong or didn't do enough of— but we recognize that it helps to at least examine some of these things as we continue to tread the path of dealing with our own son's craniosynostosis. It is our sincere hope to inspire families with our perseverance and strength, but we also want them to learn from the mistakes we made along the way.

After everything, the best advice I can give anyone facing this type of situation is to laugh as much as possible, count your blessings, and be grateful that medicine and science have come far enough to provide a solution. Keep reminding yourself that the diagnosis is not a punishment but instead an opportunity to learn. Only when the stakes are this high can you truly understand what it means to love, because ultimately real love does not differentiate between external and internal beauty—instead it lives deep in the soul, where such distinctions simply don't matter. Like our own heartbeats, real love pumps us full of purpose, giving us a reason and a chance to be better people. Real love becomes our spiritual motivation to give more and expect less; it teaches us to feel and express gratitude; and, most important, it asks us to cherish one another unconditionally.

CHAPTER 24

The Power of Information and the Art of Staying Strong

The world is full of suffering; it is also full of overcoming it.

—HELEN KELLER

Laura:

Our experience ultimately taught us that the biggest challenge facing craniosynostosis is the need to create a sense of urgency. There exists a lingering misconception that this condition is rare or random, but the reality is that it impacts approximately 1 out of every 2,000 live births. Unfortunately, because medical professionals are not sufficiently educated about the illness at the academic level, it is not on their radar when they go on to practice medicine. Similarly, expectant parents, women of childbearing age, and young adults are not educated about craniosynostosis by their GPs, ob/gyns, pediatricians, or gynecologists, so they are not empowered with the information they need to take the necessary steps on behalf of their child when he or she is diagnosed with the condition. We decided that our campaign would have to extend far beyond the scope of simply helping people. Our efforts would have to include education and dissemination of information on craniosynostosis, an illness that even some of the best doctors in the world, such as our own Dr. Staffenberg, consider to be as yet poorly researched and fertile for deeper study and advancement. As we continued to form the structure of the foundation, we needed to come up with some collective effort, one in which parents would always be prepared and doctors consistently updated and informed, a system in which treatments could take place synergistically, effectively, and on time through the power of information and education.

Not only did Dr. Staffenberg take the helm as the captain of our battle against the disease, but his insights also inspired our outreach within the foundation, a platform that can significantly better the lives of children afflicted with this illness. If the foundation acted as our new vehicle for awareness building and research, Dr. Staffenberg would now be our hero, visionary, and pioneer. His experience, knowledge, and savvy would inform our cause and campaign.

With his guidance, we started to shape our agenda more acutely, with two specific awareness initiatives: the first one was a medical poster illustrating the various manifestations of the illness for medical professionals, to be distributed throughout the country. This simple tool could educate doctors and nurses on what to look for in order to properly diagnosis (or rule out) craniosynostosis. The motivation for this initiative was to literally get this resource directly into the hands of anyone on the front lines working with infants, children, and parents, including medical students. In doing so, we could at least have the peace of mind that the relevant professionals were properly informed.

But as we continued to brainstorm the various ways of disseminating information, we quickly realized that our outreach would also have to extend to nonmedical professionals. So our second initiative was to create a "Craniosynostosis 101"

Jane Mendez (Laura's sister):

I was really impressed with Laura's maturity. She was able to separate the objective from the subjective, which to me seemed impossible, given the emotions that are intrinsic to something like this. She kept her cool, moved forward, and gathered information. She knew that she had to turn her crisis into a learning experience, and from the moment she made that mental switch, she was not going to be stopped.

pamphlet, which would essentially be available to anyone with an interest in the disease. We did this because something that always came up with families dealing with craniosynostosis was the idea that although parents instinctively knew something was not right, many times they were encouraged by their doctors to ignore it and not worry about it. This issue compelled us to provide families with sufficient information to go back to their doctors and say, "This is not something we can ignore." By having the information from the get-go, there is no chance of things slipping through the cracks.

The bottom line is that craniosynostosis can be treated, but parents need to know about the disease so that they can look out for it. Think about the long list of potential dangers that expectant parents are typically warned about, such as breech birth, preeclampsia, problems with the placenta, preterm labor, low birth weight, and stillbirth, to name a few. *Why is craniosynostosis not on that list?* If we are not afraid to talk about conditions such as Down's syndrome to a pregnant woman, we should not shy away from addressing the issue of craniosynostosis, which is just as real, if a bit less common. Although no one wants to imagine the possibility of severe illness when it comes to his or her newborn, being informed about anything that can go wrong arms parents in advance. If things do go awry, they will then have a point of reference for what is to come and in that way will waste less of their precious time and energy trying to digest the shock of it all. As we see it, information is power, and when you're dealing with something as difficult to understand as craniosynostosis, you definitely need all the power you can get.

It never ceases to amaze us how what we once considered our deepest family secret, something that even my husband and I barely dared to discuss, has today transformed into our heartfelt desire to help others in need. Our pain evolved into love, which would inevitably also affect the entire emotional landscape of how we would deal with our own son's craniosynostosis.

Some mornings we wake up and have a hard time realizing that our lives once revolved around abdominal crunches and sporting victories. Awe-struck, we are amazed that, through this experience, we have become markedly different people on a markedly different mission. Jorge Luis survived, we survived emotionally, and now it was up to us to help other patients with the disease and their families. The foundation has become our third baby; a special evergreen entity that we hope will live on, even beyond us, one that can always serve as a refuge for patients and families everywhere. It is our hope that people will always associate the Posada family with craniosynostosis and will know that our foundation is a one-stop resource for emotional and financial support. It is also our sincere hope that our own children, Jorge Luis and Paulina, will continue to carry the torch for us, so that the foundation will continue to grow and develop, keeping the fire of our cause alive for as long as humanly possible.

Over the years, so many of Jorge's fans have showed their support by sending letters to the stadium, wishing us well. Some kids who were fans even took money out of their allowances to be able to donate to the foundation, which we still can't believe. One little boy even brought his piggy bank to one of our fundraising gala events. We don't know if he himself had craniosynostosis or perhaps knew someone who did, but either way, it was one of the cutest things we have ever seen. I guess that's when it hit Jorge that being the catcher of the New York Yankees could be about so much more than just playing ball.

Another day a woman came up to me at the stadium and said, "I bought these Yankees tickets just so that I could come and meet you. I swear I am not here to watch the game." She took a photo out of her purse and said, "This is my son, and he has craniosynostosis. Can you help me?" Needless to say, my heart dropped (as did Jorge's when I later told him the story), and I very clearly understood the poignancy of our new agenda.

My grandmother used to tell us an amazing allegory. She said, "If you're eating a piece of bread and happen to look over your shoulder, you'll see someone else eating your crumbs; and if that person looks over his own shoulder, he will, in turn, see someone else eating the crumbs of the crumbs." The moral of this story is that things can always be a lot worse than you think. No matter how bad you think you have it, someone out there has it infinitely worse, an idea that helps me keep my feelings in check whenever

I am about to start feeling sorry for myself. In many ways we were lucky, as Jorge Luis's deformations, though blatantly visible to those close to him, were also subtle enough that he could pass for being "normal." There were maybe a handful of times that we got stares or comments from teasing children or even adults on the street, and thankfully, Jorge Luis was then still a baby and would likely not remember any of those incidents.

As we continued to educate ourselves about the disease, we met other children whose cases were far more severe. Many of them fell into the genetic/syndromic class of craniosynostosis (meaning that their deformities will recur even beyond the surgical corrections), which can negatively impact a life forever. Deformity, at its worst, can put a stamp of inferiority on the faces of these helpless children, who essentially begin their lives feeling shame. Right off the bat, these kids start out lacking confidence and self-esteem and instead tread their already difficult paths feeling inadequate and sad. They see other "normal" kids as lucky and themselves as victims of some cruel injustice that they have no way of understanding, much less fixing.

The other side of it is that we are taught early in our lives that human beings come in all colors, shapes, and sizes, so sometimes a subtle deformation of the skull, jaw, or chin perhaps does not register to other people (or even to ourselves) as a "problem." In many cases, especially when children are diagnosed after infancy and into childhood, the kids themselves are accustomed to their appearance and do not really have any other reference point for what "normal" is supposed to be. Sometimes the only ones who know are the closest members of the family; and in many cases parents have to sit idly by, praying that their child does not come home from school one day in tears over some snide remark from another cruel kid. We all know that kids can be mean, slashing the self-esteem of their peers left and right without even knowing they have the power to do so. And because physical appearance is such a delicate issue among children and especially preteens and teenagers, a grade school child with a deformation is likely not to have an easy time.

These kids may never feel emotionally armed to walk with confidence down the school corridor, or they may always feel too ashamed to raise their hand in class, lest they draw attention to themselves. They may not develop leadership skills, participate in a school play, or engage in relationships and social activities. They may not even know it (as in the case of those who have not been diagnosed), but they may feel that they are forever in the shadow of their condition. We know that there is no specific formula for how things will flow, and there are so many variables at play (time, the healing process, surgeries, whether the sutures begin to fuse again or not) that all we can do is watch the situation closely, monitor children routinely, pray with all of our hearts, and hope for the best.

———————

So how are we actually supposed to cope? How are we supposed to endure the possibility of our kids' potential suffering, and how are we supposed to be patient when there is a tiny little baby in our lap who, at less than ten months old, is about to have his skull opened from ear to ear? In our darkest moments, we asked ourselves if we were equipped emotionally to handle having a child with a disease that would require regular craniotomies; a child whose face was deformed from birth and who might one day be the brunt of kids' jokes in the park. We wondered if we could handle the guilt of not having any deformations ourselves or of having more kids who would be born with no complications at all. How could we show our strong and sturdy selves to our sick child, when the mere sight of him would forever remind us of his affliction? At first we could not imagine any of it; we were completely lost somewhere between shock and grief, just trying to digest and somehow accept what was being thrown our way.

But somehow, as happens in life and especially in survival mode, sorrow evolves into action. We realized that we actually *could* cope, that we *had to,* and that by doing so with as much courage as possible, we would be doing our job. We began to measure our integrity as parents by the degree of bravery and faith that we could muster and used all our will to consistently relay this feeling to our kids. No matter what the odds against us might have been, we were determined to show our best face to our Jorge Luis and Paulina, determined that our optimism would resonate with them. Despite the ambiguous trajectory of the disease, we made up our minds to stay strong so that our children would learn directly about the positive power of this unique experience that we were sharing as a group. Our hope is that they have picked up on the art of optimism so that whatever hardship (sickness or otherwise) they ever encounter will always be met with courage, strength, and faith.

CHAPTER 25

Solid as a Rock

Let us be grateful to people who make us happy;
they are the charming gardeners who make our souls blossom.
—MARCEL PROUST

Jorge:

Before I was a father, I would try to picture the way my future kids were going to look, and I know it sounds crazy, but somehow I always imagined them exactly as they are now: Jorge Luis with his straight brown hair, dark skin, and dark eyes; and my daughter, Paulina, whom I always pictured with crazy curly hair and bright green eyes. I somehow saw them in my mind's eye, and now that they are real, healthy, and happy, I feel as though the most important thing in my life has been achieved.

My first passion was baseball, until I met my wife. As a couple navigating the emotional roller coaster, Laura and I would begin to really see the beauty in love, a magical culmination of chemistry that started on a softball field (or in a bowling alley, if you ask Laura). When our son was born and diagnosed with this disease, that love was even more magnified, forcing me to view life in a new perspective. What were once two kids in love are today a pair of adults who were able to transform a burden into a blessing and, in that transformation, reinforce their bond. I feel that we have become partners in the truest sense. Through this experience, we have tapped into some kind of supersacred union that will fuel our marriage forever. I always knew there was a reason why I had to have this girl, and now, looking back at everything that has taken place, that reason is as clear as day.

My wife's fortitude was immeasurable, and her dedication to our son, and to the cause at large, continues to amaze me every single day of our lives. The love Jorge Luis has for his mother too is almost poetic. He is always looking for her, admiring her, and smiling at her. She is not only his mom, she is the love of his life. Half of the year, while I am away on the road, Jorge Luis becomes the de facto man of the house and extremely protective of Laura. He hates it when she changes her hair, he becomes annoyed when other men show her any attention, and *he even gets jealous of me!* I guess he knows intuitively that she always took care of him and instinctively feels that he owes her the same. We have some help at home, but Laura prefers to do everything herself: getting the kids up in the morning and

Derek Jeter (fellow New York Yankee):

We are very brotherly. We lean on one another for
support not only as teammates, but also as friends. Men
show support in a very different way than women do,
so I'm sure it was meaningful for Jorge to know that he
had buddies to vent to.

But I do believe that the test of a family is how you
deal with adversity. And the way they dealt with it was
by turning it into a positive. They never really had to
talk about it publicly; they could have just dealt with it
and moved on. But they chose to take it a step further
beyond their own survival, which says a lot about the
kind of people they are.

ready for school, taking them here and there, cooking for them,
everything. She is the quintessential hands-on mother.

The remarkable part about our experience is that it's not
just our own families that shaped it but also the all-around family support system that we get from the New York Yankees, very
much a brotherhood in their own right. They have always given
us what we needed, be it emotional support or resources for the
foundation to evolve. The team is really like an extended family,
another group of people who always show their love.

Our foundation also runs on the principles of any close-knit family. Each staff member and mentor family is a small link in a chain that is getting stronger and more powerful by the day. Though our objectives were clear when we conceived the foundation, as important as delivering on those objectives is our agenda to instill a sense of closeness and intimacy for everyone involved. Given the delicate nature of the illness, the fact that we are dealing with young children, and generally how overbearing the whole thing can be, we decided that positive energy would have to be the fuel on which we would always move.

Because I had to be away at games a lot or on the road for many of those most awful moments when Jorge Luis was into and out of hospitals, being with my family today makes me realize how much my presence makes a difference. I realize how much they love having me around. I realize what I can do to help, and I also realize what I have been missing while I was away.

Jorge Luis did not only teach me how to be tough and how to live life one day at a time, but he also taught me how to cherish every moment. Before all of this, I didn't have a real sense of how people could suffer. You hear all about the suffering in the world, but you don't fully understand it until you experience it firsthand. It is amazing how once you undergo pain of your own, your sense of compassion is instantly lit.

Now I relish the simple things: sitting and doing homework with my son or hearing his stories from a day at school. Imagine the joy we felt when one day, after years of wondering if Jorge

Luis would ever be totally okay, we received the following report from one of his elementary school teachers:

> Jorge is an endearing little boy with a radiant smile and
> an ever-present twinkle in his eye. He is a confident child
> who has a good sense of responsibility for himself. He
> has learned our classroom routines quickly and he always
> strives to follow the rules. Jorge cooperates and adapts
> well to changes in the classroom. His relaxed and friendly
> personality makes him popular with his peers and easy to
> get along with. Jorge has already made many friends within
> his peer group, and he relates very well to his teachers. He
> is immediately affectionate, bestowing the best of hugs on
> them often . . .

One of the things we feared the most when we were first dealing with the diagnosis was the mortifying prospect of Jorge Luis being teased at school by his classmates. We dreaded the possibility of snide comments from ignorant bullies as much as we feared the image of him sitting alone on a playground bench. Thankfully, we were lucky, and Jorge Luis was spared the potentially traumatic mockery of other kids at school. He actually turned out to be a social butterfly, developing solid friendships at school over the years.

Perhaps his life events have unconsciously taught him about

*Sue-Ann Kasdin (mother of Jeremy,
    Jorge Luis's best friend):*

Jorge Luis and our son, Jeremy, have been friends
since nursery school. They were introduced on the
playground, and from that moment, they were like little
magnets, an instant attraction right away. They have
a brotherhood type of relationship and are incredibly
loyal to each other. They have this maturity about them,
where they can just sit and talk for hours like a couple
of old souls.

For many years Jeremy mistakenly thought that he
had been the one to cause Jorge Luis's problem, because
one time he accidentally hit Jorge Luis on the head
when they were playing. Years later, when Jeremy saw
Jorge Luis with a bandage wrapped around his head
following a surgery, he became inexplicably emotional
and teary-eyed. All that time he thought he had been
the one to cause his friend's injury. I was finally able
to explain to Jeremy what had happened, and now he
really understands, as best as a nine-year-old can, what
craniosynostosis is. Though it may be true that kids can
be mean, they can also be tremendously sensitive.

the things that matter most. He has seen photos of children who were not as lucky as he, and he genuinely feels compassion for them. His maturity and sense of character never cease to amaze us, and maybe his experience has somehow taught him unconsciously about the tremendous value of being a good person—and the fact that the blessing of health is the greatest gift of life.

We tried to make our son's life as normal as possible. We would remind him of things to avoid but also wanted to make sure that he would have a memorable, happy childhood. If he wanted to climb a tree, Laura was right up there behind him, making sure he wouldn't fall. Today, Jorge Luis is as physically active as any of his peers and even has a special affinity for extreme activities, such as riding down a zip line on family vacations in Costa Rica, a true testament to his blazing courageousness. Sure, there were plenty of afternoons during the many months that lapsed between surgeries when he went to play outside knowing that he had to wear a special helmet to protect his head, which he understood required special care and attention. He would always accept this graciously and valiantly go about his business smiling from ear to ear.

Helmet or not, he is fearless; the kind of kid who is constantly up for a challenge and moves through life with a sweet and sunny disposition that people have come to adore. Granted, he knows that he was born with a problem, but, more important, he knows that it is under control. He is aware of the fact that he isn't perfect, but he will tell you himself that the most important thing is that you feel right on the *inside,* which is something we talk about a lot.

You see, after a lifetime of trying to *be* the best, Laura and I came to realize that the most worthy of all accomplishments is to actually *feel* your best. Though as kids we were accustomed to excelling physically in sports and signing modeling contracts, as adults we would learn firsthand about what really matters and learn how to re-appreciate our lives through this new perspective. We came to understand that the true meaning of success has nothing to do with professional achievement and everything to do with personal growth. We learned that beauty is only skin deep. Today Jorge Luis and Paulina wear their personalities proudly, with total confidence. Like us, they understand that their peace of mind matters infinitely more than what they look like; they understand that their smiles must come from within.

CHAPTER 26

Heart of Love

She discovered with great delight that one does not love one's
children just because they are one's children, but because
of the friendship formed while raising them.
—GABRIEL GARCÍA MÁRQUEZ

Laura:

I n our family, we have a sacred tradition, a special little ritual
we like to call "*currucki* time," from the Spanish word *acurrucar,*
which literally means "to cuddle or nuzzle." Our kids cannot
go to sleep without currucki time, and frankly, neither can we.
If we do not get this designated time of closeness, this time to
appreciate one another, we are simply not ready to end the day.
Our souls are accustomed to our daily bond, and our hearts are
always hungry for more love.

What I am trying to say is at the end of the day *it really is all about currucki time.* Family, that primal anchor of trust, is what matters most, and it is certainly what held the most weight for us as we have trodden the rocky path of craniosynostosis for the last ten years. Our kids became like oxygen to us, each moment with them a deep inhalation of love and joy. Every morning, it was their sweet little voices saying funny little things that would sound to us as the ultimate call to rise—a reason to be the best we could possibly be, whatever the circumstances. Seeing them gradually develop into little adults inspires our desire to improve constantly, to find meaning in the details of life, and to create goals that cater not only to ourselves but also to those around us.

When faced with the diagnosis, though times were undoubtedly tough, our natural instinct was to tap into our own sense of kinship, reaching back to our own childhoods in Puerto Rico. During these years we received unconditional love and encouragement from every member of our own respective families, each one a little beacon of love and wisdom for us to admire and observe. We learned from them about the power of unity, the collective strength of a group, and the innate sense of responsibility that comes with being a clan. We can acknowledge that our parents were strict, but one of the things they taught us in their firmness was the value of family and togetherness. That is the glue that has kept our bond intact. It is that miracle, the miracle of family, that fed our experience and reminded us daily of the need to persist, to keep going, to evolve as individuals, as a couple, as parents, and now also as fighters in the battle against craniosynostosis.

Even though we didn't talk about the illness a lot at home, we were always there for each other. We made it a point to spend lots of time together simply because we enjoy each other. Laughter was always a number one ingredient on our list of coping mechanisms, all of us competing with one another to entertain collectively. We learned how to quickly block negativity just by reveling in one another's smiles and company. We would eagerly look forward to our currucki time and our pillow fights and even developed another game called "king of the bed," where we throw one another off the bed, fighting for our own private Posada throne. Today, we all dress up for Halloween, we play sports together, we exercise together, we cook and eat together, and we share in one another's lives every day in every way—all of it underscored by our fundamental bond. Jorge Luis says that he is never going to go to college and is going to stay here with me; and Paulina proclaims that she will go away, but that I will go with her and we will have an apartment together as roommates! Our Paulina was born into a family in distress, and despite this harsh reality for such a little one, she was always right there with us, asking questions, keeping us company, forever wanting to know if her older brother would be okay. She was into and out of the hospital, too, but mostly as our little buddy and personal family comedian, alleviating the air of tension and unease and always trying to make us laugh.

When Jorge Luis was born, I learned for the first time what unconditional love was. In that moment I started to care about

somebody in my life other than myself and experienced feelings that I had never felt before. The woman who used to walk
around campus as if she were a cast member of *Charlie's Angels*
began to disappear, and in her place emerged a devoted mother,
a wife, a friend, and a woman with a personal cause more important than any hairstyle or career choice. From the moment Jorge
Luis came into the world, all I wanted to do was take care of
him. All I cared about was his comfort, his calm, and his delight.
His needs replaced mine, and with that he would own my heart
forever. When you finally learn what love is, the extent of what
you will do for that person is immeasurable. You become aware
of your capacity to give yourself entirely, which forces you to see
life in a whole different way. In the end, of all the people who
ever loved me, it was the love of my family that would truly win
me over.

I will never forget one time when we were flying from
New York to Tampa. I was sitting with Jorge Luis, Paulina was
asleep, and my cousin and Aunt Doris were sitting in front of us.
The plane was about to land, so the flight attendant was asking
everyone to please turn off all electronic devices, per usual. The
lights went down, and we started to make our descent. Being
the precocious kid that he is, Jorge Luis didn't want to turn off
his Game Boy. I looked at him and said, "I know you don't want
to turn off your Game Boy, but you know I love you more than
anything in the world, right? So when I tell you to do something,
it's only 'cause I want you to be okay. While you are with me,

if you listen to what I tell you, you will *always* be okay, nothing bad will ever happen." He smiled as if I had never done anything wrong in the first place and said, "I know, Mama." At that exact moment, a man with what seemed like psychological problems sprinted from the back of the airplane to the pilots' cockpit and started punching and kicking the door. We didn't know who he was or what could possibly be going on. Then a second man started running after him, screaming "Alex, don't do it!"

At that moment the plane stopped its landing and started gaining altitude again while passengers jumped up from their seats to attack the guys and pin them to the floor. The flight crew managed to wrangle him and calm him down. We learned later when we were watching the news at home that the man had recently served in the war and was suffering from some type of post-traumatic stress disorder. "Are we going to die, Mama?" Jorge Luis asked me nervously. "No, honey," I assured him, now calm myself after a quick jolt of panic. "Nothing is going to happen. Remember what Mama just told you. When you're with me, you will always be safe." I meant it that day, and I mean it every single moment of my life, and looking back, I do not necessarily think it's a coincidence that the incident occurred just as I was pledging my love to my son.

There were so many moments where Jorge had no choice but to be a New York Yankee, smile at his fans, and play with all his heart—when inside that same heart was breaking for his little boy, who was all bandaged up and swollen, recovering in some cold, horrible hospital. My husband had to put his game face on even when all he could do was think of our son's life. But he always went out there with his chin up and a look in his eye that said he would not be stopped. It was exactly the kind of strength we needed from him—and exactly the kind of strength we would always get from him.

Looking back, I have no choice but to appreciate the wondrous and divine mystery that was at work at that softball game when I was a teenager and Jorge was the umpire. Likewise, I have no choice but to be grateful for the serendipitous chance of our later encounter at the restaurant in Puerto Rico. Those moments, as I understand them now, planted the seeds of a love that would ultimately serve not only our romance but also trickle into the fabric of our endurance as we faced the challenges of our son's disease. Jorge chased me relentlessly, and despite my indifference he never gave up. This basis of commitment would later help us through the worst of times and, as I see it now, it was our very foundation. His early demonstrations of perseverance would teach me about the power of loyalty, a virtue we would mutually cling to during the darkest moments. He always devoted himself entirely to me, to my needs, and later to the needs of our children, regardless of the fact that he was a rising star in the sports world. To the rest of the world he might have been the talented catcher of a world-famous baseball team, but to us, he was our personal hero. It was his love for me that sparked the story of this family and his constancy that always served as our foundation.

––––––––––

There are two scenes that always play in my mind: the first one is that horrible moment in 2000 at the All-Star Game in Atlanta, when all of the New York Yankees got to parade out onto the baseball field with their happy, smiling children in tow. That year I had to watch my poor husband appear on that field childless. He had to fake it and run out to the field alone simply because we were not ready to show the world what our son looked like. We were simply not ready to share our pain. Despite Jorge's ability to smile through the grief, I knew that it was like a knife in his heart. He tried to show strength to his fans, to us, to his fellow players, but there was no getting around the fact that he was torn up from the inside.

I guess the universe remembered this profoundly heartbreaking moment, and maybe it is true what they say about karma, because several years later (after so many surgeries, countless tears, and an emotional roller coaster that took us everywhere on the psychological spectrum) at the Milwaukee All-Star Game in 2004, when the players were again called out onto the field, Jorge finally had his chance to show our son to the world. Instead of running out there himself like the rest of the players, he sent our son—now fully recovered—onto the field in his place. I remember the look of pure pride on my husband's face as he watched Jorge Luis parading around with the rest of the New York Yankees. His expression radiated happiness and peace, his impenetrable smile telling the world, "I am the happiest man alive."

Out in the middle of the baseball field was our little boy, healthy, happy, and confident enough to run around in front of thousands of people. Little Jorge was a little lion out there. The fans and players alike were without words, everyone crying at the spectacle of this tiny little boy with a heart the size of the stadium. Some people say it was the highlight of the All-Star Game that year. That moment was symbolic of our new life, allowing us to once and for all release our fears about what our son's life would be like and begin embracing what his amazing life was *already* like.

———————

Jorge Luis has developed wonderfully. He is alive with curiosity, dynamic in his talents, and ready to conquer the world. Gone is the little boy in the bandages whom we were once afraid to hug too tight. In his place now is a confident little boy with a smile on his face every day and enough spirit, vitality, and spunk for all of us. He has become our hero, reminding us every day about the genuine miracle of life.

Jorge Luis is very much aware of the fact that he has endured serious surgeries and is even ready for the possibility of more down the line; however, his positive attitude remains untouched. He approaches every aspect of his life with true character and sensitivity. In fact, just recently he picked up the telephone and called Dr. Staffenberg himself to tell the doctor exactly what his concerns were about his scars from the last surgery. As he matures, it is clear that he is becoming more and more connected to the reality of what it means to be a patient of craniosynostosis and every day takes a greater interest in the progress of his continuing treatment.

He may not even begin to appreciate the magic of it himself, as his experience with craniosynostosis has essentially been his life, his only real point of reference, whereas we saw the whole thing unfold from moment to moment, doctor to doctor, surgery to surgery. For us, to see our little boy running around the house today is a miracle and the kind of thing we will never, ever take for granted. He is such a solid individual, to the point that every day *he teaches us a lesson*. The other day I told him he was invited to a birthday party and asked him if he wanted to go. He was quiet, so I pushed on and asked, "Yes or no?"

He said, "Let me think about it, Mom."

I then asked, "What's there to think about? It's simple. Yes or no?"

He looked at me intently and said, "It's not simple, Mom; sometimes you say the first thing that comes to your mind but then you change your mind—so I like to think about it and give you an answer that I am going to be sure of." How could I possibly argue with that? Ironically, in school he doesn't even like to be known as Jorge Posada's son, to the point that he signs "Jorge Mendez," Mendez being my maiden name. He wants to be known for his own personality, not for the fame of his father. People ask him, "So, you're Jorge Posada's son?" And he answers, "I am not Jorge Posada's son—I am Jorge."

———————

It is hard to believe that there was a time in my life when all I wanted was a valid passport, a law degree, and perfect abs. It is difficult for me to see that selfish girl who cared for nothing but her own accomplishments. I never imagined that my greatest triumph would ultimately be a family of my own, that my children would be the two things in this world that I am genuinely most proud of. I suppose over the years I took the vigor and pep of my youth and redirected it to being the best mother that I could possibly be.

When I look into the eyes of Jorge Luis and Paulina before I put them to bed at night, I see the meaning of everything the universe has given us to handle. I can almost see our family saga unfold in a flash each time one of them blinks. Though I try to keep the saddest memories at bay, there is not a day that goes by that I don't somehow pay respect to the past. But now, instead of feeling self-pity for the deck we were dealt, I revel in the fact that precisely *because* of that deck, we were motivated to make a difference. Through deep tribulation we were forced to look at the world with new eyes and new hearts and to create a purpose for our lives that would go above and beyond our own needs. We were asked to redefine ourselves in the context of what mattered most—our family—and in that process, stormy as it was, we rediscovered love.

Acknowledgments

Our family's experience with craniosynostosis often left us feeling that we would never survive emotionally. This *gratitude* has now become a driving force of our worldview. Without this sense of profound appreciation, we would be completely lost, and we feel this indebtedness not only for the fact that we *did* survive but also for all of the remarkable individuals who stood by us, like veritable rocks of love and support, reminding us, each in his or her own way, what true compassion is all about. From relatives and friends to colleagues and fans, our path was paved with tenderness and encouragement, which made our journey less wrought with bumps so that we could arrive where we are today.

With our hearts full of love and admiration, we would sincerely like to thank the following individuals: our children, Jorge Luis and Paulina, for teaching us what it means to truly love;

our parents, Tamara and Jorge Posada, and Jeanette and Manuel Mendez, for arming us with values and education, and for always teaching us the power of perseverance; our siblings, Jane Mendez, Manuel Mendez, and Michelle Posada, for being there unconditionally through the good and the bad; Tia Doris, for lending a hand during some of the darkest hours; all of our aunts, uncles, cousins, and the rest of our extended family, for consistently coloring our lives with warmth and closeness; all of the New York Yankees, with special thanks to George Steinbrenner, Joe Torre, Derek Jeter, Tino Martinez, Mariano Rivera, and Bernie Williams for their brotherlike support on and off the field; our close friends in Puerto Rico, such as Liliana, Natalia, and Benjamin, for reminding us always that home is where the heart is; our friends Luis Espinel and Edgar Andino, our very own human guardian angels; our friends Carolina and Eyal Morad, who have shown endless love and support; Michelle Gittlen and the entire staff of the Jorge Posada Foundation, for their tireless efforts and hard work; Dr. Patrick McCarthy and Dr. Howard Weiner, for initially helping us set Jorge Luis on the path to recovery; Dr. Gerald Tuite and Dr. Ernesto Ruas, for helping us achieve the needed calm after the storm of New York; and Dr. David Staffenberg, for his endless wisdom, extraordinary talent, unconditional support, and genuine friendship.

We would also like to thank the entire staff of the Craniofacial Center at the Children's Hospital at Montefiore (CHAM); the staff of the National Foundation for Facial Reconstruction

(NFFR); everyone at the Children's Craniofacial Association; and everyone at AmeriFace.

We would also like to heartily thank all those who participate in the Mentors Program and those who selflessly donate their time, funds, and resources to our mission.

Finally, we would like to thank all of the patients of craniosynostosis and their families, not only for being some of the bravest people out there but also for helping us understand our sense of purpose with new eyes and new hearts.

Family Stories

When we began to see that families were actually being affected by the work of the foundation, when we saw that our efforts were paying off, when we realized that we could make a difference in the life of a child, we were utterly and completely blown away. We felt that we were witnessing the miracle of possibility firsthand, seeing that our trauma could have a ripple effect of positivity down the line. The momentum of growth and change was starting to feel very strong, and we made up our minds to ride that wave of optimism as we continued our work in fighting craniosynostosis not as sufferers but instead as pioneers. What was once a sense of shame and guilt in time evolved into a sense of deep pride: pride in ourselves for standing strong and making important changes and decisions and pride in our son for being such a strong little man.

Over the years, we have been blessed to meet some amazing

families with incredible stories of hope, faith, and courage as each faced off against the disease. Each of these stories empowers the potential of our campaign and reminds us that there is a bright light at the end of even the scariest of tunnels. We thought it would be appropriate to include some of the letters that we have received over the years, each of which represents a deeper resonance of our collective voice. We wanted to include them not for the purpose of tooting our own horns but instead to exemplify, through the words of others, the true power of support and strength in the face of pain and fear. Today, these words continue to remind us that our work with the foundation is endless and that it really is our job to serve as the extended family of all children affected with this disease. We encourage you to read their stories.

AT FIRST, we just couldn't believe that Nicole had been diagnosed with craniosynostosis. She was already three and a half years old. I happened to find out that she had the condition when I went to an appointment with a neurosurgeon, for my son, O'Neil, who was born hydrocephalic. I brought Nicole with me to the appointment by coincidence, and when the doctor saw her he mentioned that her forehead seemed to be a little deformed. I thought it was strange that her pediatrician hadn't noticed the deformity.

I felt my whole world turn upside down. Having one sick child was hard enough; just imagine having two. The diagnostic test had been difficult, and I couldn't imagine what the operation would be like. The worst moment for me was when they actually operated on Nicole, and believe it or not, they were actually operating on O'Neil at the same time. Nicole's operation was really something. The scar went from ear to ear. When she came out of the operating room she was completely disfigured and crying. It really made a huge impact on all of us. The good part is that we were able to overcome the situation, even though it was an incredibly difficult time.

When all of this was happening I felt very alone, and I'd had no idea that craniosynostosis even existed. I kept asking myself, "My God, why me? We don't drink, we don't smoke, we don't have any bad habits . . . why me?" After asking myself that question for so many years, I now know that everything in life has its purpose. Now Nicole is 13, she's completely healthy, and she's my reason for being. And it is because of her that I am standing here now, stronger every day. I'm very lucky. I can look back and see that the bad parts are behind me. They were sad times, but my belief in God helped me through it.

—*Peggy Chevalier, mother*

AT FIRST, I really didn't understand I had it, but as the years passed, I started to understand what craniosynostosis was about. Thank God, I'm happy now because I'm well and because I have a family that supported me through it all. Sometimes I feel bad because everyone asks me what happened to my head and I have to tell them about my condition. If I wear a ponytail or braids at school, all of my friends will ask me about it because they can see the scar.

Even though I feel bad sometimes, I also feel lucky, because as a result of this condition I have met the Posada family. Thanks to the Foundation, I've been able to learn more about my condition and how to deal with it from day to day. I'm also proud to be a source of inspiration for many of the parents that are part of the Foundation and manage to cultivate happy and healthy households. The parents see that I'm 13 and I'm doing well and it gives them hope that their children will be okay, too. Some day, I hope to become a mentor for the Foundation, so that I can help families and children that live with craniosynostosis. My dream is to be a pilot. I want to travel the world and show everyone that even though I have craniosynostosis, I can still reach my goals.

—*Nicole Perez, daughter of Peggy Chevalier*

STEVEN WAS MY miracle baby. I had previously suffered several miscarriages; so to actually carry a child to term was quite an accomplishment for me. Steven is my second child. My first son, Christopher, was born via emergency cesarean section due to the cord being wrapped around his neck. I was asleep during the entire delivery. We were eagerly anticipating Steven's birth, and I was looking forward to actually experiencing the birthing process.

At first, Steven was perfect. Then about two months later, my husband saw it. The misshapen head, the forehead that popped out like a beak, and his eyes bulging more than normal. I was too frightened at first to investigate. The pediatrician said, "Let's wait and see if he outgrows it." By the time Steven was five months old nothing had changed, and it was time to take the next step.

We saw a pediatric genetics specialist in Blythedale Children's Hospital in Westchester County, New York. This is when I heard the news: Steven had craniosynostosis. I stood in the doctor's office, frozen in fear with all of these horrible thoughts in my mind. "What exactly is craniosynostosis? What was going to happen to my son? Was he going to survive? What were the long term effects going to be?" I felt like my heart was being ripped out of my chest. All I could do was cry and hug the doctor, begging him to make Steven well. The next thing to cross my mind was "Michele, you're a horrible mother. You passed this condition to your son." The night we came home from the doctor, I couldn't sleep all night, gripped with fear, afraid for my son's life and again thinking to myself, "This is all my fault."

Once I started to calm down, I realized that I had to be strong for Steven. We had a long road ahead of us, and having a mother who was hysterical and crying all the time was not going to accomplish anything.

Now we had to face the surgery. Our surgeons made us feel as comfortable as possible regarding the severity of the surgery. They answered all of our questions, and calmed our fears as best as they could. We were as prepared as we could be, facing the unknown and putting our son's life in the hands of virtual strangers.

The surgery was a nightmare, one of the worst things a parent would ever have to go through. When Steven came out of surgery, all I could do was stare at him, hold his hands, and say to myself, "Why Steven?" He was unrecognizable from all the swelling, and all I could think was, "Please don't let him die. Please let him survive this and live a normal life." Steven was hospitalized for three weeks, having picked up a bacterial infection in the hospital. He was on IV antibiotics for about six weeks. We had to have a nurse make home care visits to give him the treatments.

Fast-forward seven years, and Steven is incredible. He is a smart, intelligent young man who makes friends with everyone immediately. He is an orange belt in karate, and learned to ride a two-wheel bicycle at four years old. The scars from his surgery are virtually unrecognizable. He truly is my Miracle Baby.

—*Michele Connelly, mother*

NATURE SURPRISES US, even after all of our technical advances, every day. I am the mother of a six-year-old child who was diagnosed with craniosynostosis. As a mother, I would see Hector day after day, and I started to notice that his motor skills and his intellectual capacity were not normal for a child his age. Faced with this situation, I set out to find alternatives with which to help my son. My son received the necessary resources right away when diagnosed with craniosynostosis. The process required an emergency operation to correct his cerebral growth. As his mother, the process has been a long and exhausting experience, but the enthusiasm and joy I get from seeing my son regain, little by little, his quality of life has been the greatest reward for all of us. I think our society drives us to instill a spirit of independence in our children. I will provide my son with all of the help he needs for his physical, mental, and emotional development at every stage of his life. The craniosynostosis diagnosis has helped us to value life even more, and has brought us together as a family. The support group that my son is seeing is exceptional, and we work together, contributing to a society that helps itself and others. I give thanks to God, the doctors that operated on Hector, and the great support group of the Jorge Posada Foundation.

—*Yasmin Morales Rosa, mother*

WE WENT INTO our son's journey with many fears and questions. Before Peter's surgery, we met with the team of experts: a neurologist, a craniofacial surgeon, and an anesthesiologist. These miracle workers answered and explained in detail what each doctor's role would be.

On the day of Peter's surgery we could not hold our child close enough, knowing we had to hand him over to these strangers, not knowing if we would see him again. As a mother, my last word to the anesthesiologist when handing him our son while crying uncontrollably was "Promise me our son will wake up."

As first-time parents and a mother who was told she would never bear her own child, it broke our hearts to find out our six-month-old baby would have to undergo this incredibly complicated surgery. All of our struggles with infertility and our disappointments and heartaches would never compare to the way we felt knowing our little baby had to endure this journey.

The Jorge Posada Foundation always had someone to answer our questions and calm our fears. Our mentor provided us with a detailed account of his family's personal journey. The Foundation gave us confidence and provided us with the strength to face our own challenge head on.

—*Nina Mottolese, mother*

THIS WAS THE QUESTION I asked my wife: "Who will help us?" We knew, after our son was diagnosed, that we would be facing economic expenses that were beyond my income. Thank God that many doors opened for us. One of them—the most important and helpful one—was the Jorge Posada Foundation. Through the Foundation, our son has been able to receive his treatments and surgeries in the United States. In addition to covering the costs of housing and travel, their unconditional support has been a blessing for us. Today, Ederyk is a completely happy child, and my wife and I are even happier. God bless the Posada family and their staff. We appreciate their strong sense of responsibility, their careful attention and dedication, and their support for these very special children.

—Henry Medina, father

OUR SON WAS DIAGNOSED with a severe case of Metopic Craniosynostosis two months after he was born in 1998. Despite the obvious emotional turmoil, our focus quickly turned to finding a pediatric plastic surgeon who could "fix the problem." During our search, we were referred to Dr. Frank Vicari at the Children's Memorial Hospital in Chicago.

We were already aware of the wonderful reputation Children's Memorial had worldwide but kept an open mind when we walked into the doctor's office for the meeting. Within ten minutes, we both knew he was the one who would perform the surgery. He had a genuine confidence about him, which convinced us that the man knew what he was talking about, and that everything would be all right. We also discovered that he was a professor at the Northwestern University Medical School who had performed thousands of these surgeries, and his reputation within his peer group, both local and national, was nothing short of outstanding. He was the top in his field and our minds were made up that day. Joe's surgery was a huge success and today, at age nine, he continues to excel in school and sports. But most importantly, he still smiles all the time.

—*Beth McCormick, mother*

"**WHY IS THIS** happening to me?" I asked myself when they told me that Gian Carlo needed an operation for craniosynostosis, a condition that we didn't have a family history of. He was our first son and the first grandson in our family. During the course of Gian Carlo's operation, I asked lots of questions and found out that in some families it affects many of the children and spans generations, and in other families it is an isolated condition, like in our case. If I have another baby, how do I know it won't happen again? But, I became pregnant again when Gian

Carlo was only eleven months old. Just five months after he'd had his craniosynostosis operation. I didn't have time to think about or consider this so that I could decide whether to get pregnant. My other baby was already on its way.

The first question I had for my gynecologist was "Gian Carlo has craniosynostosis, how do I know if this baby has the same condition? Is there any way to see it in a sonogram?" The answer was no; you can only see it in the last weeks, and even then only in very severe cases. What calmed my husband and me was seeing Gian Carlo's rapid recovery and how well his operation went. Only God would know how our next baby would be born. I had to wait, and those nine months of waiting were very long.

When Natalia was born, the first thing I looked at was her head, to see if I could see anything different about it. Everything looked okay, and I thanked God, because at least this baby wouldn't have to also go through this experience. For the first few months, I looked at her head constantly to be sure it was growing well. My experience with Gian Carlo's craniosynostosis made me uneasy about other babies' heads. I can't help but look at a baby's head to see if it has some deformity, and if I see one, I ask myself, could it be craniosynostosis? Should I tell the mother, or would that be bad?

As a mother, I can't help but wonder why Gian Carlo was born with this and what the cause is. I wonder about the future, and about whether his children will have the condition. All I can do is wait and hope that with advances in science and the work of the Jorge Posada Foundation, someday we will know what causes craniosynostosis.

—*Margie Alvarez Gierbolini, mother*

———————

MY SON, Hector Gadiel Ramos, was born with craniosynostosis. Thank God he feels fine, and now that he is already a 14-year-old adolescent, he says he feels at peace. We live in a housing project in Rio Piedras and the children here tend to be very cruel. Because Hector's head is slightly deformed they tease him and call him names. Hector is very intelligent and the things they say to him haven't affected him.

Every day I tell him that he is different than other kids, but that he's fine. I tell him that he's healthy, he can walk, he can eat, that he has all his fingers and toes, and that he has legs. I remind him that there are many people in the world worse off and who have had much heavier burdens to carry in life. I tell him all the time that he has to get on with his studies and with his life. I also make him understand that he shouldn't feel inferior because of this condition, because inside he is just like all the other children.

A short while ago a psychologist evaluated Hector and she told me that his self-esteem was strong, and that the results place him at the intelligence level of a 16-year-old. This makes me feel extremely proud of him, because it means that he has been able to overcome his condition and that all of the things I have told him, in an effort to help him with his condition, have worked.

—*Lourdes Andino Alicea, mother*

Positive Affirmations

Every family is different, as every case is different, and no two groups of people will handle this type of situation in exactly the same way. But after everything we've been through, and after all of the families who have shared their stories and experiences with us, we can attest firsthand that there are some very specific things that we can keep in mind as parents dealing with craniosynostosis or any serious illness or tragedy.

Over the years, we have developed a list of simple words, utterances that serve as little reminders to gently lead us to a brighter, more positive mental place. When we feel overwhelmed by an ominous situation, we pull out this list. We try to shelve the scary words that might be thrown at us, such as "severe" and "complicated," and instead reach down into our hearts, looking for the power of these words to re-inspire our attitude with hope. Just by trying to focus on what the words mean, you can gently urge yourself toward a better place.

Acceptance

Honesty

Compassion

Communication

Support

Initiative

Positivity

Acceptance is the acknowledgment of reality as it is, not as we would like it to be. It is our inner nod to the universe that expresses our understanding of our circumstances exactly as they are. When we finally accept, we place ourselves on the starting line of the journey ahead of us and make the mental room for the needed planning. And guess what? Acceptance is not just relegated to families dealing with illness—in fact, every single one of us must face the truth about acceptance, and *accept acceptance* as one of the primary tools of human survival.

Observe the situation, and understand that it is not a punishment from God. Accept the fact that things like this happen all the time, and then accept that you have to do something about it. Instead of wallowing in grief and the questions of why this is happening, we want to inspire families to expend their mental and emotional energy in being their own advocates within the medical community. We want them to rise up from the grief and learn more about the illness, and what they can do to better the lives of their children.

Honesty is the ideal that we, as parents, should always aspire to in all matters regarding our children—especially in the face of an illness such as craniosynostosis, where major surgeries become the norm for children who are barely old enough to tie their shoes, let alone understand what a craniotomy is. With honesty, we can calmly explain the facts to children in a language that they can understand, always talking them through every step of the way. Being honest with a child shows him respect and demonstrates to him that you are his best friend. It allows him to trust you, to put his faith in you, and to know with certainty that he will always get the bottom line from you.

Compassion is our ability to tap into our own sensitivity as we deal with the people in our lives and all of the circumstances that they bring. We exercise compassion when we, for example, put ourselves into other people's shoes; when we look beyond the horizon of our own ego and relate to the suffering of others as if it were our own. With compassion, we tell those around us that we understand them and that we care; and when we are dealing with serious illness of any kind, compassion needs to flow in every direction. Were it not for compassion, we probably would never have created the foundation, which we today consider one of our most important accomplishments.

Communication is the open platform on which everyone shares. In sharing, we express our feelings, opening up our sensitivity to a higher plane of understanding. Communication, in many ways, opens the doors to compassion, allowing us to truly understand what another person is feeling. Much of the work that we do with the foundation is based on the premise of open and constant communication—communication among all the mentor families involved, among the doctors on board, and certainly among the family members who are facing the disease. Communication forces us to share the flow of information so that, as a family, we can all be on the same page and show our support with more might.

The most significant lesson that you can communicate to a child diagnosed with craniosynostosis is that true, lasting beauty is on the inside and physical appearance is just one superficial layer of the ever-complex nature of a person. Communicate the importance of respect, tolerance, and the noble virtue of simply being nice.

Support is the fruit of our concern and compassion in action, lending a hand however it can. When we show support, we give strength to those who receive it from us; and when we receive it ourselves, we get the emotional cushion we need as we metaphorically land on the harsh reality of the illness. Support is tangible, laying itself out like a warm blanket to whoever needs to be enveloped in its comfort; and it works symbiotically, allowing both the giver and the receiver to greatly benefit from the circular flow of care and love.

Initiative is the spark that lights up inside us, compelling us to take action. It is the fire ignited by our spirit, which ultimately does not want to suffer and needs some kind of relief from the pain. For us that relief came in the form of raising awareness for the cause and in helping patients and families with the illness in whatever way we could. Our initiative forced us to get creative about how we were going to spend our energy and time. It made us realize that our task at hand was directly linked to the challenges we were facing and so energized our mission with an incredible momentum and drive. Through the power of initiative we found our strength and courage where our fear once reigned—and with that strength we have been able to make a difference.

Positivity is the sunshine inside each and every one of us. It is the active choice to be happy no matter what hardship may come your way. Positivity is that glass–half–full attitude that gives the soul what it needs to move forward. With a positive mind-set, we begin to clear the head of all the emotional clutter left by sorrow, cleaning the spirit of the negative residue that wants to hold us down. A positive mind-set does not allow itself to be held down, and fights like a lion to keep energy up at all costs. One guaranteed way to tap into your positive mental space is to look deep and start counting your blessings; when you consciously take stock of all of the things that you are profoundly grateful for, you gradually disempower the ones that bring you down, because true gratitude, in its purest form, is immensely healing.

By saying these words to yourself every once in a while or, better yet, every day, you gently remind yourself of your own power. You rekindle the positive qualities within you that will need to blaze on as you continue to face off against the disease. Remembering these words helps forge the collective energy of faith and hope and softly guides you and your family toward a solid optimism. Something I always like to remember is an adage Dr. Staffenberg once said to me: "No medical school can beat or teach a mother's instinct." So always trust your instinct, because as a parent, you will always know when there is something wrong.

Resources

The Jorge Posada Foundation
www.jorgeposadafoundation.org

Our website and the Mentors Program both serve to provide the best and most accurate information about the myriad of considerations: from doctors and hospitals to before-and-after photos, insurance coverage, the surgery, and what to expect. We provide information and connect families who have gone through the process with families who are at the very beginning of that road.

As part of our agenda, we have also joined forces with many fantastic organizations, such as AmeriFace, a group whose mission it is to provide information and emotional support to individuals with facial differences and their families. Additionally, we work with the Children's Craniofacial Association, a nonprofit organization dedicated to improving the quality of life for people with facial abnormalities. CCA's mission is to empower and give hope to individuals and families affected by these types of conditions.

As we continued to develop our own foundation, we quickly saw the need for resources and medicine in places like our own home, Puerto Rico. There, such an illness barely registers on the medical radar, and sadly, many children are left undiagnosed and untreated. This made us realize the need for a wider global effort to bring this understudied illness to the fore.

Today, we also partner with a slew of wonderful medical centers, such as the Children's Hospital at Montefiore, New York University Medical Center, the Yale School of Medicine, and Centro Medical Hospital in Puerto Rico. Through these medical centers we can assist families from all over the world with the costs of surgeries and treatments, underwrite innovative and groundbreaking teaching tools for surgeons all over the world, and sponsor academic and professional summits for domestic and international medical professionals. During these medical symposiums, physicians from every corner of the globe are invited to learn about craniosynostosis and share their own country's experience with the illness. Imagine how stunned we were to find out that some insurance companies in Italy do not cover the cost of these reconstructive surgeries, claiming they are cosmetic procedures. Needless to say, our conferences help to dispel such thinking, the idea being to convene the best and the brightest to ensure communication and collaboration on a global level so that we can create best practices and standard protocol worldwide.

There are many craniofacial centers throughout the United States, and though now we're just touching a few, our goal is to go international. Our ability to make this kind of impact comes through our work with the National Foundation for Facial and Cranial Reconstruction, specifically in the development of a virtual surgical teaching tool that will be distributed to more than 50,000 doctors globally.

In the 1990s, Dr. Court Cutting, the plastic surgeon famous for his work on cleft lip and palates, began the development of this virtual surgery project, which was essentially computerized graphics that served as a model of a head during surgery. Though it was possible to rotate and revolve the heads on the animations, it was still limited, because doctors, of course, couldn't actually open up the skin and look inside. Dr. Cutting, who was a brilliant mathematician as well as a brilliant surgeon, started working with a highly advanced software tool called Maya, an Academy Award–winning program used in many Hollywood films, which allows for powerful, integrated 3-D modeling, animation, visual effects, and rendering. Applying this software to virtual surgery, Dr. Cutting added a new dimension of possibility to the practice of these very delicate procedures, making it possible to open the skull virtually and look inside. He essentially wrote new software that would allow doctors to mimic surgery and create topological changes. Using a scrimlike layer over the animated model, he was able to show the skull of the patient, in the context of how a normal skull should be, to show where the aberrations and

Dr. Court Cutting (professor of plastic surgery,
New York University Medical Center):

I can't go to India to operate on every kid who has a
cleft lip and palate issue. It makes more sense for me
to work with the local doctors there who are very good
and just need to be brought up to speed and introduced
to some of the more modern techniques. Using these
virtual teaching tools, we can go through the different
types of surgeries, and instead of those surgeons having
to do it on an actual patient, they can do it on a
computer simulation.

Aside from being a teaching tool at large, the
virtual surgery project is also applicable on a per case
basis. You have to consider that facial deformations are
all very unique, simply because faces are all so different.
Variables such as age also come into play, because
younger children have tighter skin, while older skin is
more elastic, etc., the point being that every surgery is
going to have its own particular set of circumstances.
Let's say, for example, that a plastic surgeon designs a
unique solution to a craniofacial problem; first he will
identify the topological change they want to make, and
then he will inevitably ask questions, such as: Will this
portion of skin reach over and cover this defect? Do I
have to find a different skin graft to cover this hole?—
and the effectiveness of his plan will only truly be tested
after these questions are answered.

There is nothing worse than going into the operating room with a plan in your head that you think will work and you start to cut—only to realize that your supposedly brilliant plan is flawed. The beauty of this tool is that doctors can virtually move the skin in whatever manner required, to experiment and practice with their ideas and plans before they actually perform the surgeries. If a patient needs certain types of facial implants, for example, and the doctor has various options in mind, in a virtual environment he can actually try them all and see which ones work best *and* look best. And with this type of development, we basically turn an art project into an engineering project.

One of my colleagues likes to tease me and says that I'm taking all the romance out of plastic surgery. But as far as I am concerned, plastic surgery is not worthy of art; it's really a craft, one that calls upon the artistic method to solve facial reconstruction problems.

inconsistencies were and to see how much that skull needed to change or be altered in order to fit a normal profile.

Dr. Cutting showed each stage of a surgical procedure, so doctors could memorize and learn them, as he says, "as test pilots who learn in simulation and not on a plane carrying 250 passengers."

The main purpose of the Jorge Posada Foundation is to reach out to families in need whose children are affected by craniosynostosis and provide them with emotional support through the foundation's family support network. The foundation provides financial assistance to underwrite a portion of the costs of initial surgeries in partner medical centers throughout the United States. The foundation also raises awareness about craniosynostosis through educational outreach and events. Through targeted partnerships with various medical centers, the foundation assists families from all over the world with the costs of surgeries and treatments; underwrites innovative and groundbreaking teaching tools for both domestic and international surgeons; and sponsors academic and professional summits for domestic and international medical professionals.

Jorge Posada Foundation Complete Mission

- To raise awareness about craniosynostosis and ensure that medical professionals and parents are aptly informed—because if doctors and first-time parents do not know that an illness such as this one exists, they will certainly not be adequately armed to deal with any of the challenges that come with dealing with it.

- To administer an effective Mentors Program, which connects families dealing with craniosynostosis with one another, with the goal of sharing information, experiences, resources, and support, so that those who are at the beginning of the journey have the benefit of insight from those who have already gone through the process.

- To sponsor family conferences and events, such as the North American Craniofacial Family Conference and the Children's Craniofacial Association's Family Retreat.

- To provide grants to and partner with medical centers to increase their capacity to provide pro bono surgeries and underwrite associated costs, such as the Children's Hospital at Montefiore; the Institute for Reconstructive Plastic Surgery at New York University Hospital through NFFR; Connecticut Children's Medical Center Foundation; and Winthrop Medical Center.

- To sponsor yearly educational seminars for pediatricians, such as the 2008 Craniosynostosis Symposium in partnership with Montefiore Medical Center; along with a symposium in Puerto Rico, led by Dr. Staffenberg, where it was our goal to educate fifty pediatricians about every aspect of craniosynostosis, as we discovered that many children on our own home island were not being diagnosed in time, leading to additional complications down the line.

- To develop medical posters and pamphlets that explain craniosynostosis to help educate medical professionals working on the front lines with newborns, babies, and children.

- To partner with the National Foundation for Facial Reconstruction to develop a virtual teaching tool to be distributed to 15,000 doctors in third-world countries and throughout the United States.

- To provide a grant to rehabilitate the craniosynostosis surgery recovery room at the Centro Medico Hospital in Puerto Rico.

- To host events such as the annual Heroes4Hope Gala in New York City and the Celebrity BaseBowl Tournament in Puerto Rico.

AboutFace
www.aboutfaceusa.org

This organization's mission is to advocate on behalf of those touched by facial differences with peer connections, information, and emotional support and help create opportunities to enhance their life circumstances. It is also dedicated to changing attitudes and dispelling myths about facial differences through the media, school community, and general public. Ultimately, its vision is to create a society that is accepting and welcoming of differences so that every person can be valued and able to achieve his or her full potential.

AmeriFace
www.ameriface.org

The mission of AmeriFace is to provide information and emotional support to individuals with facial differences and their families and increase public understanding through awareness programs and education. The organization supports individuals whose facial differences are present at birth, as well as those who have acquired facial differences as a result of illness, disease, or trauma, such as stroke, cancer, accident, or burns.

Children's Craniofacial Association
www.ccakids.com/index.asp

Children's Craniofacial Association is a nonprofit organization dedicated to improving the quality of life for people with facial differences and their families. Nationally and internationally, CCA addresses the medical, financial, psychosocial, emotional, and educational concerns relating to craniofacial conditions. CCA's mission is to empower and give hope to individuals and families affected by facial differences.

The Craniofacial Center at the Children's Hospital at Montefiore
www.montekids.org/services/leadership/craniofacial/

The Craniofacial Center at the Children's Hospital at Montefiore (CHAM) boasts an exceptional multidisciplinary team of specialists that has made it one of the most respected craniofacial programs in the world.

Cranio Kids
www.craniokids.org

This website was started by a mother and father who sought information on craniosynostosis when their own son was diagnosed with the illness. They wanted to create a forum that would be family-friendly and upbeat but that would also provide the critical information needed to get through the disease. The goal of Cranio Kids is to create a caring and educational environment where families can go for support, friendships, and fun.

Craniosynostosis and Positional Plagiocephaly Support
http://cappskids.org
http://www.facebook.com/group.php?gid=24655514785

The primary goal of this organization is to raise awareness through education. Although these two conditions are very different in cause, in many cases they have a similar outward appearance, which causes many misdiagnoses. By educating the health care community and general public, it aims to reduce the amount of misdiagnoses so that children will receive the appropriate treatment for their condition without loss of valuable time. Its secondary goal is to offer support to families that have a child with either condition.

Craniosynostosis Support for Parents and Guardians on Facebook
eo-eo.facebook.com/group.php?gid=16254297457

This is an excellent and convenient way to participate in discussions with other parents and exchange stories with people who might be going through the exact same thing.

FACES: The National Craniofacial Association
www.faces-cranio.org

FACES: The National Craniofacial Association is a nonprofit organization serving children and adults throughout the United States with severe craniofacial deformities resulting from birth defects, injuries, or disease.

Forward Face
www.forwardface.org

The mission of Forward Face is to help children and their families find immediate support to manage the medical and social effects of facial differences. They work to educate, advocate, and raise public awareness about craniofacial conditions.

Institute of Reconstructive Plastic Surgery (IRPS)
http://surgery.med.nyu.edu/plastic/

The mission of the Institute of Reconstructive Plastic Surgery (IRPS) of the NYU Medical Center is to maintain a leadership role in local, national, and international plastic surgery by providing the highest standards of patient care, by offering optimal educational programs, and by organizing clinical and basic science research programs.

Johns Hopkins Center for
Craniofacial Development & Disorders
www.hopkinsmedicine.org/craniofacial

This website has a great resource section linking visitors to a number of sites dealing with craniofacial conditions.

KidNeeds
www.kidneeds.com

This is a resource children with special needs, families, and others can consult for comprehensive information. Here you can find professional opinions on important topics, learn about public health policy and advocacy efforts, link to programs and services, connect with other caring families and friends, and purchase a wide range of products specifically tailored for children with special needs in one simple-to-shop place.

The National Foundation for Facial Reconstruction
www.nffr.org

The National Foundation for Facial Reconstruction is the non-profit, fund-raising arm of the Institute of Reconstructive Plastic Surgery (IRPS), which provides treatment and support for those who are born with or acquire a craniofacial difference.

Medical Q&A with Dr. David Staffenberg

Following are frequently asked questions, answered by Dr. David Staffenberg:

Q: *What exactly is craniosynostosis?*

A: Craniosynostosis describes the condition when the joints (or sutures) between the separate bones of the skull fuse together before they are supposed to, causing a growth disturbance. This is typically manifested as some sort of unusual head shape. Think of it this way: "cranio" = skull; "syn" = joining; "ostosis" = bone. In normal development, the sutures—which you can think of as the grout between the tiles—drift apart, and the "grout" starts to fill in with new bone. When we stop growing normally, the brain stops growing and the plates are no longer pushed apart, so the sutures fuse. In craniosynostosis, long before growth is complete, those bones get stuck together. This restricts the expansion of the brain in a certain direction. As the growing brain needs more room, it pushes further in other directions. Craniosynostosis may involve the premature closure of a single suture or multiple sutures in the case of a syndrome. The words that describe the resulting head shapes of single-suture craniosynostosis are as follows:

- Scaphocephaly = elongated, narrow skull

- Plagiocephaly = flattening of the skull
  (usually on the front and/or back)

- Trigonocephaly = triangular head shape

Q: *How often does craniosynostosis occur?*

A: Generally speaking, craniosynostosis occurs in at least one out of 2,000 live births and affects males twice as often as females. As is true with other medical disorders, the incidence appears to increase as awareness grows. This phenomenon is illustrated by the following: in the last year I have traveled to a small but sophisticated country to take care of babies with craniosynostosis. Until my visit to take care of the first severe case, doctors there felt that there was no craniosynostosis. After my lecture to pediatricians, they found that they did indeed have babies with craniosynostosis and in subsequent visits I have taken care of babies with both simple and complex craniosynostosis.

Q: *What is the most common type of synostosis?*

A: The most common kind of synostosis is when the middle of the skull—the sagittal suture—is fused. If that happens, the growth of the skull to the left and the right is limited, forcing the brain to push toward the back and front of the head. These children end up with a very narrow and long skull, almost shaped like a canoe (doctors call this shape "scaphocephaly," which derives from the Greek *skaph,* meaning "boat"). Craniosynostosis is called "simple" when only one suture is involved and "complex" when two or more sutures are involved.

Q: *What are some types of craniosynostosis?*

A: Following is an overview:

Unilateral coronal craniosynostosis involves fusion of either the right or left coronal suture that runs down each side of the forehead. This interferes with the normal growth of the forehead. This produces a flattening of the forehead and the brow on the affected side. In order to compensate, the brain pushes the other side of the forehead out, causing it to be excessively prominent.

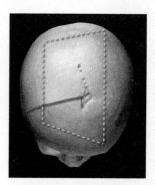

Unilateral Coronal Craniosynostosis

The eyes also appear to have different shapes. There may also be flattening of the back (occipital) area due to further compensation.

Sagittal craniosynostosis occurs when there is fusion of the sagittal suture, which runs from a spot at the front of the head to the back of the skull, resulting in a long, narrow skull with or without bulging of both the back and front of the head. The narrowing begins at the back of the head first since the suture closes

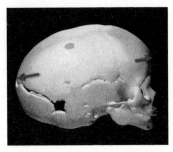

Sagittal Craniosynostosis

from back to front. In babies with a lot of hair, this may be difficult to see. In our experience these babies are more likely to be diagnosed by their parents during hair washing.

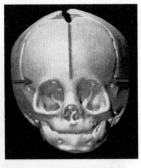

Metopic Craniosynostosis

Metopic craniosynostosis results in a narrow, triangular forehead with pinching of the temples laterally (referred to as trigonocephaly). The metopic suture runs from the top of the head down the middle of the forehead, toward the nose. Early closure of this suture may result in a prominent ridge running down the forehead. Sometimes the forehead looks pointed, like a cone or triangle, with the eyes placed closely together (hypotelorism).

Bicoronal craniosynostosis causes brachy-cephaly. This occurs when both of the coronal sutures fuse prematurely. Characteristics include a wide-shaped head with symmetric flattening of the skull, and the fusion prevents the entire forehead from growing in a forward direction, causing a tall, flattened forehead.

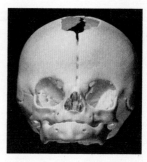

Bicoronal Craniosynostosis

Multiple suture synostosis occurs when all the sutures are fused. In these more complex cases, there is greater concern about the possibility of increased intracranial pressure and other associated anomalies. These babies will generally require a more complex treatment plan that may include multiple surgeries throughout their childhood. In the most severe cases the only growth will be that which is accomplished through surgery. In these complex cases, synostosis of multiple sutures, including those in the facial skeleton, will indicate the need for facial surgery as well in order to improve breathing, protect the eyes, and keep the teeth in better alignment.

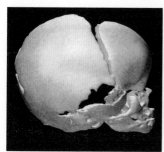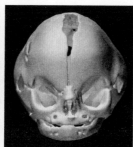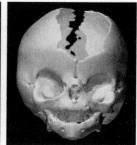

Multiple Suture Synostosis (there are several examples, as depicted through Apert, Crouzon, and Pfeiffer syndromes, pictured from left to right).

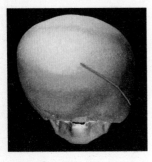

Metopic Craniosynostosis

Lamboidal synostosis is perhaps the most rare form of simple craniosynostosis. This condition arises when sutures on either side of the back of the head close prematurely, which leads to posterior plagiocephaly. This will cause flattening of the back of the head on the affected side, protrusion of the mastoid bone, and posterior positioning of the affected ear. It may also cause the head to tilt sideways.

Q: *If left untreated, what is the worst-case scenario for patients of craniosynostosis?*

A: Craniosynostosis can cause severe and permanent damage. An infant may have increased intracranial pressure, seizures, neurological problems, eye problems, and misalignment of the spine, as well as cognitive and developmental delays. But these types of assessments are not always so simple.

Q: *What causes craniosynostosis?*

A: Complex molecular mechanisms are the cause of craniosynostosis. These mechanisms are being studied in an effort to enable more reliable early diagnosis and perhaps to offer additional lines of treatment.

Q: *In the hereditary cases, how is craniosynostosis inherited?*

A: In some families, craniosynostosis is inherited in one of two ways:

- **Autosomal recessive:** This means that two copies of the gene are necessary to express the condition, one inherited from each parent. In cases where both parents are carriers, there is a 25 percent chance, with each pregnancy, of having a child with craniosynostosis, with boys and girls being equally affected.

- **Autosomal dominant:** This means that one gene is necessary to express the condition, and the gene is passed from parent to child with a 50/50 risk for each pregnancy, with boys and girls equally affected.

Q: *What is the goal of the treatment plan for craniosynostosis?*

A: In the simple cases, we aim to do one single operation to get the presenting issue fixed, with the hope and goal that the child will not need anything else. In the syndromic/genetic cases, however, we understand that these babies are simply not programmed on the molecular/genetic level to grow normally. In these cases, all the sutures start to fuse, so the skull itself will not allow the brain to grow. As the brain grows, the skull bones are "locked in," so the problems become severe and include restricted brain growth, blindness, loss of hearing, neurological problems, severe facial deformations, and even death. In these cases, we cannot fix all of the problems in one operation because the ensuing growth will still not be adequate. But when we do see them as newborn babies, we can already have a sense of what is likely going to happen over the next sixteen years and we can lay out a treatment plan with the parents during their first visit with us. The treatment plan may need to be adjusted as the baby grows since growth will not be completely predictable. The good news for these patients is that we can also start to develop a strategy and attempt to have all the surgeries mapped out, keeping a close eye on how rapidly these things change, so that the timing and technologies of the operations can change along with them. Even more good news is that the simple, nonsyndromic, single-suture cases of craniosynostosis far outnumber the genetic cases. There is no question that the genetic cases are real long-term projects, but families dealing with these types of cases should find some solace in the fact that there are also viable treatments and solutions available to them, especially when craniosynostosis is diagnosed early enough. The relationship that we develop with the babies and their parents is very important from the very first visit.

Q: *How is craniosynostosis diagnosed?*

A: In 90 percent of cases, we can make the diagnosis by examining the child. We often have families who walk into our offices holding a folder of records, CAT scans, MRIs, and X-rays; they will come in with the baby on their laps, and I'll ask, "Who first identified the craniosynostosis?" Stunned, they always ask, "How did you know?" They think the medical records are going to tell me what I can plainly see with my own eyes. But I can see it only because I am trained to look for it, which is why it is so important to raise awareness about this disorder. The more doctors know the disease well, the more quickly and effectively will children be diagnosed and treated properly. X-rays, CAT scans, and MRIs may not be necessary, so we recommend that these studies be requested only based on the results of a consultation with an experienced craniofacial physician.

The interesting thing about craniosynostosis is that it is not going to be diagnosed unless it is already in someone's mind, and there is a scarcity of doctors who have ever seen (never mind studied) this particular illness. Amniocentesis may be performed during pregnancy and may identify a genetic case, as we see plenty of families with syndromes that are associated with craniosynostosis, such as Crouzon syndrome (which presents with wide-set, bulging eyes), Apert syndrome (which presents with fused fingers and toes), Pfeiffer syndrome (which presents with broad, short thumbs or big toes), and Jackson-Weiss syndrome (which presents with enlarged or bent big toes), to name a few. In these families, the syndromes recur even after they are treated, telling us that the synostoses are clearly part of a genetic scenario. Exactly what genes are involved and how they are passed down through families is still being studied. However, what is known is that if a couple has a baby who develops craniosynostosis, there is a small risk that any future children that they conceive together will also develop the condition. This risk is estimated to be between 1 and 4 percent.

Q: *What happens if we don't treat patients with craniosynostosis or they are not treated in a timely fashion?*

A: When we do miss the opportunity to operate on these kids, when we miss it early in the game, later on we are concerned that we may see these children begin to lose their vision, for example; or we may notice that they are no longer reaching their developmental milestones. These are the things that we constantly race against to correct up front. We never want to be too aggressive by subjecting the babies to unnecessary risk, but if we are not aggressive enough, the hurt will be greater down the line. So it is like walking a tightrope, and there is no real formula or recipe to follow. When planning surgery, we constantly assess risk versus benefit and try to keep the benefits of surgery large while minimizing the risks. Interestingly, we must weigh the risks and benefits the same way when *not* performing surgery.

Q: *What are some things your doctor might do to examine your infant for craniosynostosis?*

A: First, your doctor will take a careful look at your baby's head and face, including the position in which your baby holds her head. Then he or she may:

- Measure the circumference of the baby's head

- Take photographs

- Request a computed tomography (CT) scan of the head

- Request an MRI

- Perform genetic testing on the parents

- Answer your questions

Q: *What are the symptoms of craniosynostosis?*

- An unusual head shape, as discussed above; this is the most common symptom

- A full or bulging fontanelle (soft spot located on the top of the head)

- Sleepiness (or less alertness than usual)

- Very noticeable scalp veins

- Increased irritability

- High-pitched cry

- Poor feeding

- Projectile vomiting

- Increasing head circumference

- Seizures

- Bulging eyes and an inability to look upward with the head facing forward

- Developmental delays

Q: *What is the differential diagnosis of craniosynostosis? Are there other conditions that craniosynostosis can be mistaken for?*

A: Because of the potentially invasive treatment for craniosynostosis, it is vital to ensure that the diagnosis of craniosynostosis is accurate. This is important because there is another condition that it can commonly be confused with. This disorder is called deformational plagiocephaly, which some people call flat-head syndrome or positional plagiocephaly. In craniosynostosis, the head shape occurs because of an intrinsic problem, an internal action on the bone; whereas in deformational plagiocephaly the issue is extrinsic. It occurs, for instance, in babies who have been wedged tightly in their mother's pelvis, which may have molded the head shape irregularly; those are the ones that we can treat without surgery if we recognize it in the proper time frame. The tricky part is that we should not have to rely on the

CAT scan. We have to be able to quickly distinguish between an intrinsic skull problem (craniosynostosis) and one that occurs on the extrinsic level (deformational plagiocephaly). Because again, for the babies who do require surgery, we need to get moving in that direction at the right time. We do not have a three-year "grace period" to sort it all out.

Back in the 1990s, the difference between craniosynostosis and positional plagiocephaly was poorly understood. The American Academy of Pediatrics proposed the Back to Sleep Campaign in order to reduce the incidence of SIDS, where parents were encouraged to place newborns on their backs in the crib, with no loose bedding. This decreased the incidence of SIDS but perhaps caused flattening of the back of the head. This is clearly a very small price to pay in order to avoid SIDS, but deformational plagiocephaly must be recognized when it occurs.

Another example: if a baby is always put on her back and she always needs to turn her head to the right in order to watch *Barney the Dinosaur,* which is playing on a television across the room, over time the back of her head will slightly flatten according to her "watching" position. It will deform because of this external pressure. For this reason, we tell parents to turn babies in the crib (head to toe and side to side), making sure that they live every which way while they are little, as this is when they are most amenable to correction. Corrective helmets can also be used to treat more severe cases of deformational plagiocephaly (or those diagnosed later).

Following is a chart that breaks down the differences between deformational plagiocephaly and craniosynostosis:

	DEFORMATIONAL PLAGIOCEPHALY	CRANIOSYNOSTOSIS
Shape of head:	When viewed from above, the skull appears to be shaped like a *parallelogram* (forehead and/or back of head is flat)	When viewed from above, the skull appears to be shaped like a *trapezoid* (forehead and/or back of head is flat)
Caused by:	Repeated pressure to same area	Cranial sutures that fuse closed too soon
Premature fusion of cranial sutures?	No	Yes
Diagnosis:	Physical exam (CAT scan in questionable cases)	Physical exam (CAT scan in questionable cases)
Treatment:	Positioning, cranial remolding helmet or band	Surgery

Q: *When is "the right time" for surgery to correct craniosynostosis?*

A: In a best-case scenario, we want to get the surgery done as early as it is safe, because it minimizes the secondary growth problems, but we also know that when we are in surgery manipulating bone, it needs to be strong enough to hold the reconstruction. The structural demands of the proposed surgery vary according to the specific type of synostosis. But in some cases operating too early is a bit like building a house if the wood is not yet strong—it simply may not hold. In all cases, there is a plus side and a minus side, and our job is to try to keep everything in balance. We observe the patients' progress over the years and start seeing and looking for patterns: we ask ourselves questions such as "What seems to do well when we operate at x months versus y months?" And it is not just the safety and outcome of the surgery itself that we are looking at but also the details of the surgery itself: Is there a difference in the amount of time in the operating room? What about the exposure to anesthesia if we operate at six months versus two or three years of age?

Q: *How do doctors develop treatment plans for patients of craniosynostosis?*

A: The key to dealing with craniosynostosis is accurate, early diagnosis and medical treatment. Be sure to bring your infant for regular doctor's visits, so your pediatrician can routinely chart the growth of your infant's head over time. Communicate any concerns about your baby's head shape to your pediatrician, which will help to identify the problem early, if it occurs, and then specific treatment will be determined based on:

- Your child's age, overall health, and medical history

- The type of craniosynostosis (which sutures are involved)

- Expectations of the course of the craniosynostosis

- Your opinions and preferences; be sure to ask questions

Q: *What kind of medical team should I assemble to treat my child's craniosynostosis?*

A: The important members are the plastic surgeon and the neurosurgeon in the OR; the anesthesiologist; and the surgical technicians, who hand us what we need without us having to ask for it, so that we don't need to take our eyes off the patient. There must also be an experienced team in the pediatric intensive care unit to treat these babies afterward, because they require a very special type of post-op care. Parents often ask why both a plastic surgeon and a neurosurgeon have to be there, and the answer is that the neurosurgeons are the ones with the best ability to disassemble the affected parts of the skull and then the plastic surgeons are the ones who reconstruct the skull in the desired fashion; this will take future growth into consideration. A craniofacial team includes a geneticist, a speech therapist, a dentist, and an ophthalmologist. While these are the specialists that are most commonly listed on a craniofacial surgery team, they will usually have access to many other specialists in their hospitals. In some cases, your baby may also require the assistance of an occupational/physical therapist.

Q: *What is the goal of the surgery to treat craniosynostosis?*

A: The goal of the type of surgery we do to treat craniosynostosis is threefold: to relieve any pressure on the brain; to make sure there is enough room in the skull to allow the brain to properly grow and the child to properly develop; and to improve the appearance of the child's head. The main procedure of the surgery is to remove all the bone causing the deformation, reshape it, and frequently use the child's own bone to reconstruct the skull. During the procedure, the incision is hidden in the hair over the top of the baby's head so that it is not visible once healed. The skin is dissected away to expose the skull. We use special instruments to work with the bone. The bone above the eyes (called the bandeau by craniofacial surgeons) may also need to be removed to allow for reshaping. When we reconstruct the skull, the baby's own bone is the best material available, and it is frequently held together with dissolvable (or resorbable) plates and screws or resorbable surgical thread. Once the bone heals, the plates, screws, and threads dissolve.

To close the scalp, we use more dissolvable thread, and a bandage is usually placed. Some surgeons use drainage tubes that will be removed later. When additional bone is needed for the reconstruction, the bones that have been removed can be split into an inner and an outer layer. That means we do not have to use anything but the child's own bone. We feel that it is important to use the child's own bone, so that the body will recognize it and not reject it.

Following surgery, most children experience only very mild pain, but it is common for them to develop swelling of the scalp or around their eyes, which can often prevent them from opening them. Usually the swelling is minimal right after the surgery and peaks on the second or third day. Though the child may find this annoying or distressing, the swelling presents no health risk, and it should go down over the following days.

The things that we worry about most during the surgery are continued bleeding and air embolism. Air embolism is when air actually enters through the veins or bone itself and travels through the veins to the heart. If an air bubble gets stuck in the heart, blood can't get past it, and that can be very dangerous. It is also important for us to be able to operate on the bone without injuring the brain or eyes underneath. Problems after surgery that can occur suddenly or over a period of time include:

- Fever (greater than 101 degrees F.)

- Vomiting

- Symptoms of headache

- Irritability and a change in the baby's sleep schedule

- Redness and swelling along the incision areas

- Decreased alertness and symptoms of being tired

These complications require prompt evaluation by the post-op pediatric team as well as your child's surgeon.

Q: *How do you know when it's all over?*

A: The most important thing following surgery is to monitor patients. In the vast majority of cases, the postoperative recovery is quite smooth and uneventful. I take care to perform the surgery in such a way that parents do not need to become nurses or doctors in order to care for the baby. The one thing to be most aware of is the fact that with the swelling of the scalp your baby's head will feel heavier and require more support than it did when he or she was a newborn; this period usually only lasts a few days. However, even in the simplest cases, where everything goes smoothly, I still ask to see the child every year while he or she is growing. A child with craniosynostosis requires frequent medical evaluations to ensure that the skull, facial bones, and brain are developing normally. In cases of plagiocephaly, head position needs to be followed carefully. The medical team really needs to work with the child's family to provide education and guidance to improve the health and well-being of the child. I personally do not like to close the book no matter how confident I am until the child is fully grown, at about sixteen or seventeen years old. I like the parents to feel a sense of assurance and to know that they are not going to be abandoned and that they will have direct contact with me for any new questions or concerns. The most rewarding part is that we usually see these babies growing well, without any problems. For me, the best visits are when they come and there is nothing to talk about except sports and summer plans. Because in a best-case scenario, when the "bad" suture has been removed and reconstruction has been done well, recovery usually goes incredibly well. The only visible scar is the scar in the hairline, which is usually covered nicely as the hair grows and the child ages.

With the more syndromic cases (the ones where problems recur even after surgeries), we know we have to entertain a more elaborate treatment plan, staying ahead of the primary and secondary problems before they arise and, as I mentioned before, carefully studying changes. These cases require serious maintenance, which, although intense for the patients and the families, we can today still thankfully do.

This brings up the emotional aspect of confronting this illness. I deal with it by spending time with the parents. They come in so anxious, and the only thing that helps is not rushing, talking about everything, allowing them to ask questions, giving them information, and being honest with them. Reassurance goes only so far, though. You have to let them digest and process all of the steps. In some cases, it helps them to speak with other parents who are going through it, and the Internet has made it easy for them to find one another quickly, and frequently they find their doctors that way. The information has to be explained clearly, in simple language; it has got to make sense to the parents. When a mother calls me and thinks something is wrong, I always listen and want to know more. It is important not to keep a distance. I also like to lay it all out and explain all the scenarios. The most important thing that parents must understand is how incredibly unpredictable this disorder can be. Patience and planning go a long way in the battle against craniosynostosis.

For some reason, craniosynostosis did not "appear on my radar screen" in medical school. But as an intern, I was poking around in the medical library, probably hiding from my chief resident, and was flipping through the pages of a book when I stumbled upon some photos of a craniofacial operation, and I was completely and utterly blown away. I sort of intuitively felt that this was for me and there was something important and far-reaching about this field, and that for the rest of my life I would dedicate myself to its study and practice. I began to see this type of surgery as creative engineering, understanding that the combination of a procedure and the passage of time could effect a physical outcome for the life of a child. In time I began to see that there was, of course, the human side as well and how when you treat these babies and develop a relationship with the parents, you essentially become the one who makes the problems go away in a very tangible, visible way—so the relationships with the families end up going pretty deep. Today, it is very important for me to show medical students what we, for some reason, were not privy to in medical school. Because with a disease like craniosynostosis, the combination of the right doctors and the right surgeries at exactly the right moments has the power to change a young child's life for the better—forever.